Prologue

Life is a story, and we all have our own special one to live. Some of us are in the early chapters, struggling to figure out the plot, while others are mired in the middle with too many obstacles and unclear dialogue. Still others are contemplating their grand, final act. You, like me started out somewhere, with your own special location, culture and passions. You're supporting cast; family, friends, neighbors, teachers, mentors, colleagues, and employers, even someone you may have casually met in passing influenced your thoughts, values and decisions. The result of these influences lead you to where you are right now, holding this book, reading these words, at exactly this moment. While our stories are peppered with our own individuality, surprisingly, they are not that unique. The specific situations are varied, but we've all experienced ups and downs, joys and sorrows, days when we were sure we could fly, and mornings when the mere thought of getting out of bed was seemingly the most painful task we had ever faced.

I see the quizzical look on your face, wondering what these "life story" mutterings are all about, swearing that you had purchased a cookbook. Let me assure you, this is a cookbook, and in it you will find a vast array of delectable recipes that will invigorate your palate and impress your friends. You see, these recipes make up one of my most important supporting characters in my life: food.

Introduction to Passion of Cooking.

This is my second book, the first one I went into detail about my life struggles, family, successes and illness. My first book was full of pictures this book is full of recipes. The first thing you need to know about me is I am a survivor. If you want to read about how I survived difficulties in my life then read my first book. This book I want to keep focused on my passion and my cooking.

Passion of Cooking
Author
Joe *Marsola* Eidem

The views concepts, and opinions expressed in this book are solely those of the author and are not intended to reflect or represent the opinions or beliefs of any other person, persons, or organizations.

ISBN – 13 – 978-0615978291
ISBN – 10 - 0615978290

Chef's words of wisdom
Passion is overwhelmingly important for success. You really can't just have an end goal, the whole process from start to finish must make you happy or else you will not be working at your best.

Go out and live your passion.
Be proud of your heritage and your family. Never deny who you are. Hang the American Flag on all holidays. Go to the church of your choice at least twice a year. Listen to your parents, you will find out they really were right. Don't be embarrassed to "hug" a friend.

Above all, be true to yourself, and if you cannot put your heart in it, take yourself out of it. Being happy doesn't mean that everything is perfect. It means that you've decided to look beyond the imperfections.

Life begins, Passion follows

Passion is important, without it is very hard to be motivated. You need passion to drive you through the road blocks every time you are learning something new. With passion it is no longer work it becomes a joy and your passion and joy will motivate your staff and all those around you.

You need passion for what you do to give you the strength to tough out the hard days at work. The secret to success with our family, our lovers and our staff is communicating with **Passion**. **Passion** is not just a philosophy or program and it most certainly it is not a soap opera. Passion is the focus energy you bring to everything you do in your daily lives.

Having **passion is important** to having a good life and being happy? What are you **passionate** about? **Passion** is a very **important** element in our life. It may make you happier or have a better life, if you are **passionate** about your job, you will enjoy an amazing career. Your **Passion** will impact your staff, your customers, your patients and your administration.

Passion comes through whatever you're medium of communication. **Passion** can spark catalytic change because it has the unique ability to generate energy. And energy forward even when you are not present. When you are so in love with something, you are so behind something that the energy just sparks off of you, when you walk in a room, at work or play you energize everyone around you that is *Passion* at work.

Let's Cook

A collection of Recipes

I use very basic ingredients, as you will see. Most of the recipes can be done with very little prep work and the cooking methods are simple. I truly believe that in today's world we just don't have the time to cook and prep all day. In most families, the husband and wife both work and neither have the time or energy to prep for hours before the meal. Also, may I make it very clear that cooking is not 'women's work'; never was and never will be. Some of the greatest chefs in the world are men, so guys get up and help with the meal!

Start the Meal

Check your recipe before you go to the store; make sure you have written down all the ingredients. While at the store, buy just what you need; if the recipe calls for one tomato, buy just one. It took me a while to learn that you can cook for less than 30 people, my wife states I always cook for 30 even if there was only the two of us. So learn to cook for the amount you are serving.

Spices: I use oregano, basil, parsley, white pepper, bay leaves, Cajun seasoning, seasoning salt and Salad Supreme seasoning. Also you should have Dijon mustard, Worcestershire sauce, Tabasco sauce, and of course, crushed minced and/or powdered garlic. Garlic is a must in most of my recipes.

Extra Virgin Olive Oil: A must! I spent some time in New York and learned so much about olive oil and all the different countries that produce it. I would recommend you take some time and study about this wonderful oil.

Red Wine Vinegar: Great in salads and salad dressings. But when you need vinegar for pastas, I then recommend Balsamic vinegar, the taste is much stronger -- like the difference between extra virgin olive oil and regular olive oil.

Marsala Wine: This is the best wine to use for cooking. I never use 'cooking wine' as there is so much salt in the wine. One of my favorite saying is, "I always cook with wine and sometimes I even put it in the food". Marsala is a dry, yet sweet wine with lots of fruit flavor. I use it in everything, it's just wonderful. If you don't have Marsala available, then use any drinking wine you might have.

My cooking methods are rather unconventional compared to other chefs, but I believe you will find them easy and delicious.

Measuring is important when you first start out as a cook, but as you get more experienced, you will find that your taste will take over and you will start measuring by the palm of your hand. This should work well if you don't overdo it, always remember a recipe is a guide. You may add more or less of your favorite vegetables, such as mushrooms, as you will not find many of my recipes include mushrooms, why? Very simple, I personally hate mushrooms. This doesn't mean they are not good, it just means I personally don't like them, and use them only occasionally. Bottom line be creative when cooking. Make cooking fit your life style and your taste. This is what is important and adds to the pleasure of cooking.

Garnishing your plate is as important as having a clean plate. If you serve your meal on a dirty plate, all the work and prep time has just gone out the window. The same applies to the presentation of your meal. Plan your meal. Do all the colors match? What are you garnishing with, a parsley sprig or a bay leaf? Maybe you want to be creative and make a rose out of a tomato skin. Either way, make sure your plate is color-coordinated and garnished well.

No matter who you are cooking for, everyone eats with their eyes first, so make the first impression the best. From the salad to the dessert, presentation must be first when planning your meal.

Table setting is as important as meal presentation. Place the fork on the left of the plate, the knife (blade turned to the plate) on the right with the spoon to the right of the knife. Match your centerpiece for your dinner and always be sure your glasses are free of spots.

Kitchen equipment can get very expensive, so shop around. I find buying at restaurant supply stores gives me high quality at less expensive prices than you would find at large department stores. I buy Teflon-coated fry pans: 6" for eggs and omelets, 10" for sauté. I keep a few saucepans for stews, broth, etc. Of these pans, it depends on how much cooking you do and how large a party you have planned. Of course I have very large stockpots. The main thing, be creative!

Be sure that each meal is full of joy and happiness. After visiting Italy, I learned that the Italians eat the main meal of the day in the afternoon between 1 and 4 PM. They just don't believe in fast food. And they share the afternoon with family and friends. After lunch they rest and around 4 PM they return to work until 7 PM. In the evening they have a light supper and retire.

When I went to Italy, I thought that most Italians would be somewhat overweight, but I found with their eating habits they were in great shape. They used very little cheese and fattening ingredients compared to Americans. They use only low fat mozzarella cheese on their pizza with lots of vegetables. They also eat lots of fresh fruits and fresh breads. So I think if we look at our eating habits, we will find that we eat too much high fat foods and too many snacks.

Working in a hospital kitchen with dietitians I have learned to cook with less fat, and yet retain the flavor of the recipe. For example, in the making of sauces, I use 2% milk instead of heavy cream, light cheese instead of regular high fat cheese, lemon and/or orange juice for sweetness, and stay away from butter and animal fat (prime sources of cholesterol).

I understand the difficulty of weight loss and maintenance as I struggle with being overweight myself, so I'm certainly not the best person to give advice on how to lose weight.

I found one of my downfalls is eating fast food, so cook at home more often, and if you are eating out, make the right choices. Stay away from the high fat items on the menu, and "Good Luck!" We all need it. As for wine, my saying is, "I judge my wine by the friends I am with, so tonight I am having very fine wine".

I truly enjoy sharing my meals and my wine with good friends and I have been blessed with very good friends. Many I have met and many I will soon meet.

Garnishes

A garnish can be as simple as a sprig of a fresh herb— the touch that sets off the food and tantalizes the eye. All it requires of the cook is a few minutes of time and a little imagination. Often, the simplest garnishes are the most elegant. When you choose a garnish, consider four things: color, texture, shape and taste.

For example, if you need a touch of green with a hearty pasta dish, fresh basil leaf may be a natural choice--it has a solid, shiny appearance, and a robust taste. With carrots, feathery dill has the flavor and texture that balances the weight of the carrots. Another way to use garnishes is in the repetition of a theme: if you used fresh thyme in a dish, save a few sprigs to decorate the top. Your garnishing arsenal is limited only by your imagination. Check out your garden or the produce section of your grocery store with a open-minded eye and browse cooking magazines for inspiration.

The old standby of orange or lemon twists is available year-round, which helps to account for their popularity. For a twist on the traditional, use a knife to peel a lemon apple-style so that you end up with long, spiraling strips of peel. Use these to bundle asparagus spears and serve with broiled or poached fish.

Lemons are a natural with foods that need a tangy twist, like fish, but they're not the only option. Try cherry tomatoes--whole, quartered or sliced--or spruce up your broiled fish by topping with fresh chives anchored with a slice or two of lemon or tomato.

Citruses aren't the only fruits you can use. Let seasonal fruits add sparkle to your meals. A slice of kiwi adds a delicate green and an interesting pattern. Try partnering it with grilled steak or chicken. Blackberries are a luscious deep purple and have an irresistible texture that makes them great with all kinds of desserts.

Strawberries are a natural garnish for anything chocolate, but don't neglect them with main dishes, too. They're perfect with breakfast entrees of omelets or pastries and also add a kick to quiches.

Vegetables too are welcome garnishes, and they don't have to be carved by a master craftsman. Carrots, squash, zucchini, peppers of all shapes and heat levels, tomatoes, radishes, broccoli, cauliflower, beets--these can be sliced, julienned, grated, curled or left whole to provide color and accent on the plate.

Use a vegetable peeler to remove colorful strips from squash, carrots or zucchini and sprinkle them on a plain-looking entree.

To make carrot curls to float in a soup or top a casserole, slice a carrot lengthwise into thin slices with a a vegetable peeler. Steam the carrots with a tablespoon of water in the microwave for thirty seconds. They'll go limp and be easy to curl and drape on a plate or dish.

While fruit and vegetables can be colorful and exotic, the garnishes I turn to most often are made from herbs. I use thyme, sage, rosemary, chives, basil, dill, sorrel, salad burnet, chervil, oregano and mint as well as parsley.

How to use them? Tuck a sprig under vegetables or in a casserole. Top a platter or individual plates of pasta with leaves or bunches. Sprinkle chopped herbs on fish or meat or floats them in soups.

Chives, for example, have an elegant form that complements simple meals. I like to lay two or three long leaves on the edge of a plate or platter or cross them on top of a dish. For a whimsical touch, use them to tie bundles of julienned carrots or green beans. Chopped, they grace soups, or you can just float an inch or so of the tips and add a dollop of cream to hide the base.

Nothing else tempts the eye like the dessert cart, yet it's often not the actual food that does the tempting. It's the decoration. Consider a basic cheesecake. A plain, triangular slice is tasty but definitely lacks curb appeal. Add a raspberry sauce drizzled over the top and artfully spilling onto the plate and you're on your way. Throw in a few fresh blueberries and raspberries tumbling down the sides, tuck in a mint leaf or two and you've got something that is all but irresistible.

For dessert at home you may not want to go that far, but don't overlook the impact of a few berries or nuts adorning the plate of something even as simple as ice cream.

Edible flowers shine as dessert garnishes--make sure, of course that no herbicides or pesticides have been used on or around any flower you plan to eat. Miniature roses or rose petals are the perfect companion for delicate desserts like mousses. Pansies add a touch of fanciful color to cakes and nasturtiums a peppery accent to fruit desserts.

Just remember, you can have too much of a good thing. You don't have to surround the plate with a border of green; a sprig can have an equal, if not greater effect. Don't lose the beauty of the dish in an overabundance of ornamentation. Above all, let the food speak for itself

Appetizers

Appetizers are great for parties, but normally I don't fix many appetizers, maybe a small plate of meats and cheese, something like an antipasto, which is assorted meats (capicola, salami, pepperoni and ham) and cheese (provolone, Swiss, cheddar). You may also add sweet peppers, olives (Kalamata or green), and anything else you might enjoy from your favorite Italian market.

A fun appetizer is made with won ton skins. You can fill them with almost anything and serve them hot or cold everyone will enjoy them. Also stuffed cherry tomatoes are very good. As for the stuffed mushrooms, well you know how I feel about mushrooms, but most people love them (Go figure!).

Soups and Salads

The beginning of the meal must be as good as the end. It is very important to prepare the soup and salads carefully ~ plan your presentation well.

On the East Coast as in Europe, you will find the salad course served after the meal. On the West Coast, it is served at the beginning.

Use very fresh lettuce, and a variety such as romaine, iceberg, and butter lettuce for a nice presentation. Garnish the salad with a tomato rose or fresh basil leaf.

For a special presentation, you might try the following: Trim the top off a bell pepper and remove the seeds. Set the pepper upright on a serving dish. Stuff the pepper with three types of lettuce -- stems down, leaves up and fanned out. Make a slit in the pepper behind the lettuce leaves and place a piece of lavosh bread in the slit. This will hold the lettuce leaves up. Drizzle the salad dressing around the pepper. I use a raspberry dressing for color.

Hints for soups ~ serve them in a small hollowed out mini pumpkin or squash. Place the lid on and have your guest remove the lid for a 'bowl' of hot soup. *Great presentation.*

Be as creative with your soup and salad as with your main meal. This is the beginning of what your guest will anticipate for the rest of the meal service. Each course must be better than the last. Don't let them down always set your goal to exceed expectations.

Entrees

This is where you can shine and get very creative. Be sure to plan each course carefully. My mother used to love to visit for the holidays, and I would tape the holiday dinner menu to the refrigerator door. This not only helped me to stay focused, but also helped me picture each course and how to present the meal. The family could also see the menu daily, and anticipate the feast.

Be sure when you plan your menu that you plan for color. For example, you wouldn't want cauliflower and mashed potatoes served together. So, after you have your menu planned and written down, start gathering your recipes, and prepare your shopping list. Just remember to stay focused on your list and eat before going to the store or you will buy everything in sight and your list will get lost in your stomach. And don't forget garnishes.

Never serve the same item twice, for instance if you use shrimp in the salad or appetizer you don't add it to the entrée'. With each entree you should serve a wine that will complement the course, I could write a book on just wine. But to make it simple, just think of the old rule "Red wine (Merlot), with red meat and white wine (Chardonnay) with poultry and fish". With pasta you should serve Chianti.

Plan your plate well. Arrange it to compliment your main course.
Finally an important thing to remember is more is not better. A
smaller serving not only looks better, it tastes better.

Vegetables
I didn't include the best and easiest recipe for vegetables, which is to
just steam them. Broccoli, Cauliflower, Brussels Sprouts, and Carrots
are wonderful when steamed. But please, don't overcook them.

Remember al dente, firm yet tender, for the best results. After
steaming, add a dash of Salad Supreme. Just don't ruin them by
smothering them in butter or other fat.

Several recipes in this section are fun and interesting, and I hope you
enjoy not only preparing them, but eating them as well. Of course, for
the best flavor, home grown fresh is the best. In Nevada, that can be a
real challenge, but in Oregon, we started to grown more vegetables
than we could eat. My dad once said when he saw my garden, "You
could plant a tooth pick in this ground and have a tree in the morning".
Well, he was nearly right. We did grow everything and enjoyed all the
vegetables. I miss those days in Oregon everything seemed so simple
back then. My youngest son Chris would dig for the potatoes and find
the smallest ones, while Tony and Bryan would remove the corn and
take them ear by ear up to Valery to blanch for the freezer. Then there
was the year that my pet goat got into the garden and ate everything.
I didn't know who Valery was going to kill first, the goat or me.

Desserts

I have never been much of a dessert person, two scoops of vanilla ice cream placed in a microwave for 15 seconds is just great for me. Now Valery is much different. She would rather skip the entree and eat just the dessert. Not me, give me the main plate and skip the dessert.

One of my favorite desserts, naturally, is Cannoli, a Sicilian dessert ~ basically a pastry shell filled with ricotta cheese. I just love them and I know a wonderful little bakery on Mulberry Street in New York that makes the best ones in the world -- next to mine, of course.

After Cannoli, my favorite dessert is Banana's Foster, probably because one of the main ingredients is vanilla ice cream. Rent-A-Chef served it all the time. I think everyone loved it as it is a light dessert and was perfect after a large meal. I would flambé at table side. It's a great dessert for parties or romantic dinners. Pastry takes a very special chef. The pastry chef must know chemistry. You can't just throw the ingredients together as in a sauté, you must measure each ingredient carefully as there is a chemical reaction that will make the pastry either rise or fall. So remember, when preparing pastry recipes you must follow the directions exactly as written or your product will not turn out the intended way.

There are several cookbooks that offer pastry and baking. I'm sorry I can't give you much advice in this category. We just never made pastries around our house or Papa Joe's. Aunt Mary made the best cakes for all the family functions.

I did take a class on cake decorating and did very well, but I will leave the decorating to wife, Valery as she is more creative than I am and she does a beautiful job. For the Christmas holiday, Valery makes a gingerbread house and on Christmas Eve the kids and I would break it and eat all the goodies. Traditions are great!

Another way of serving vanilla ice cream that is really fun you take a white plate, cover the bottom with raspberry or strawberry jam (no seeds) besure to line the entire bottom of the plate. Then place Cake Mate icing in a tube and carefully place three or four lines across the plate. With a toothpick run a line up and down the icing and you should have a beautiful decoration. Next place a scoop of ice cream on the plate, a fresh mint leaf and some fresh sliced raspberries or strawberries. You can also use a low fat yogurt for a healthier dessert and still have a great presentation.

day is a learning experience, never think you know more than anyone else.

You *don't* have to cook fancy or complicated masterpieces - just **good food** from **fresh ingredients.**
— *Julia Child*

Just some good information

Recipe Measurements
3 teaspoons = 1 tablespoon
4 tablespoons = 1/4 cup
5 1/3 tablespoons = 1/3 cup
8 tablespoons = 1/2 cup
10 2/3 tablespoons = 2/3 cup
12 tablespoons = 3/4 cup
16 tablespoons = 1 cup
1 tablespoon = 1/2 fluid oz.
1 cup = 8 fluid oz.
1 cup = 1/2 pint
2 cups = 1 pint
4 cups = 1 quart
2 pints = 1 quart
4 quarts = 1 gallon

Simple definitions you should know

Baking - is defined as cooking food in an oven using dry heat.

Al dente - In Italian the phrase means "to the tooth "and is a term used to describe the correct degree of doneness when cooking pasta and vegetables.

Béchamel - is a creamy basic French white sauce is made by stirring milk into a butter-flour mixture called a roux. The thickness of the sauce depends on the proportion of roux to milk.

Braise - a cooking method where meat or vegetables are first browned in butter and/or oil, then cooked in a covered pot in a small about of cooking liquid at low heat for a long period of time.

Bouquet garni - a little bundle of herbs, tied together or placed together in in a piece of cheesecloth, used to enhance the flavor of a soup or stew.

Emulsify - means combining two liquids together which normally don't mix easily. The ingredients are usually oil or a fat like olive oil or egg yolks, and another liquid like water or broth.

Ganache - A combination of chocolate and cream, melted together slowly.

Marinade - refers to the liquid foods marinate in' Contains some acidic liquid like lemon juice or vinegar to tenderize the foods, and may contain spices or herbs to add flavor.

Mirepoix - a mixture of diced carrots, onions, celery and herbs that has been sautéed in butter or oil and used to season soups and stews.

Mise en place - This technique is IMPORTANT and one that's hardest to get novice cooks to stick with. It's a French term for having all your ingredients prepped and ready to go before starting your start cooking. That means everything is cleaned, peeled, chopped, diced, measured out, whatever's necessary to get the ingredients ready prior to preparing your dish.

Roast - To cook by heated air, usually in an enclosed space such as an oven or barbecue pit, but also on a revolving spit before an open fire. Roasting nearly always refers to meats.

Roux - is a mixture of butter and flour, cooked until bubbly. It can be browned very deeply, then used as the basis for gumbo, etouffe and brown sauce. If not browned at all, it is the base of bechamel, veloute, or white sauce.

Stock - also called broth or bouillon, a flavorful liquid made by gently cooking meat, chicken or fish (with bones) in water and used for making sauces, soups, glaces and can be used for braising or poaching.

Appetizers

Ants on a Log
Kids just love it.
Ingredients
• Celery sticks
• Peanut butter
• Raisins
• Adult assistant to help with cutting

Directions: Wash the celery and cut it into pieces (About 5 inches long). Spread peanut butter in u-shaped part of celery, from one end to the other. Press raisins into peanut butter. There you have it.... Now you can enjoy your Ants

Bacon Swiss Dip Recipe
Ingredients:
4-6 pieces cooked bacon, chopped
8 oz. soft cream cheese
1/2 cup mayo
2 tsp. Dijon mustard
12 oz shredded Swiss cheese
2-3 chopped scallions
1/4 cup toasted almonds

garnish: paprika

Directions: Mix ingredients together in a small baking dish, top with paprika. Bake at 350 for 20-30 minutes

Eggs in Bed
This is a great recipe to introduce the frying pan when your child is ready. The bread helps absorb any grease "pops" that can burn. An egg is a difficult thing for a first-timer to flip without it ending up a scrambled mess. The bread is an anchor for the egg making it easier for the child to flip without losing the egg.
Ingredients:
One slice of bread
One Egg
Butter
Directions: Heat the frying pan on medium low. Drop in a dollop of butter. (Enough to coat the frying pan when melted). You will know the frying pan is hot enough when the butter has fully melted. Keep the temperature on medium low so the butter will not burn. As the butter is melting break a hole in the center of the bread. Enough to form a circle about the size of a golf ball. When the butter has melted place the bread in the pan. Crack your egg and drop it into the center of the bread that you have taken out.
Allow to cook until the egg begins to turn white and the bread is nicely toasted. When one side is done flip the bread and the egg to toast the other side. When both sides have been browned and the egg is cooked through (the entire clear part of the egg should be white with nothing runny remaining) it is ready to serve.

Easy Kids Pizza
What you will need:
Bagels or English Muffins
Pepperoni sliced
Pizza sauce (Hunts)
Cheese (Mozzarella and Cheddar mix)
Directions: Have an adult cut the bagels or muffins in half. Spread pizza sauce all over each half. Lay the pepperoni on top and cover with cheese. Have an adult put them in the oven until the cheese is all bubbly. You can also put anything you like on top, like veggies or other meats

---

Creamy Cheese Grits
Ingredients:
5 cups water
1 teaspoon salt
1 1/4 cups uncooked quick-cooking grits*
1/2 (8-ounce) block sharp Cheddar cheese, shredded (about 1 cup)
1/2 (8-ounce) block Monterey Jack cheese, shredded (about 1 cup)
1/2 cup half-and-half
1 tablespoon butter
1/4 teaspoon pepper
Directions: Bring 5 cups water and salt to a boil in a medium saucepan over medium-high heat. Gradually whisk in grits; bring to a boil. Reduce heat to medium-low, and simmer, stirring occasionally, 10 minutes or until thickened. Stir in Cheddar cheese and remaining ingredients until cheese is melted and mixture is blended. Serve immediately. Makes 6 to 8 serving

Guacamole Dip
Ingredients:
2 ripe avocados, peeled, mashed
(about 1 1/2 c.)
2 tbsp. cilantro, chopped (optional)
1 tbsp. lime juice
2 tbsp. of your favorite salsa, Hotter is better.
1/2 tsp. ground cumin
1/4 tsp. salt
1/4 tsp. garlic powder
Tabasco to taste
Directions: Mix all ingredients very well, serve chilled. Combine all ingredients. Cover; chill. Makes about 1 3/4 cups

Hot Salsa Dip
Ingredients:
1/2 - 1 red onion, diced
1 whole tomato cut into small chunks
1/2 - 1 teaspoon garlic powder
1 can hot Ortega green chile, diced
2 teaspoons chopped cilantro
Directions: Place onion and tomato chunks into a bowl. Add garlic powder and mix. Stir in the Chile and cilantro and mix well.

Salsa Mexicana
Ingredients:
3 ripe tomatoes, chopped
1/2 cup chopped red onion
1/2 cup fresh cilantro, chopped
4 to 6 chiles verdes (chile serrano), finely chopped, seeds removed
2 teaspoons salt
2 teaspoons lime juice.
Directions:

Mix well all ingredients in a serving dish. Salt to taste. You can, of course, make your salsa as hot as you want, by adjusting the amount of chile serrano you use. Now remember this is the basic recipe, so you can get very creative. Add diced Avocado and just a little of the Habanero Chili Pepper (if you like it really HOT).

Remember that exposed avocado oxidizes in a short period. So cut it just before serving. To prolong its good looks, keep it in close contact with its seed. Sprinkling it with lemon juice helps. If you avocado is not ripe and still hard, place it in a warm oven for 5 or 10 minutes and it will ripen very fast.

Tomatillo & Avocado Salsa

Tomatillo-avocado salsa is a great introduction to tomatillos because it is so easy yet so full of that characteristic tart, fruity flavor. Tomatillos, literally "little tomato," actually are not tomatoes at all but is a close relative. Ripe tomatillos have a dry, papery husk.

Ingredients:

1/2 pound tomatillos

2 tablespoons chopped red onion

1 Serrano chile pepper, seeded, chopped and seeds removed

1 clove garlic, crushed

1 tablespoon lime juice

1 tablespoon chopped fresh cilantro

1/4 teaspoon salt

Directions:

Peel brown husk from tomatillos; rinse. In medium saucepan, cook tomatillos in small amount of boiling water. Reduce heat to medium; cook 8 to 10 minutes or until soft. Drain. Place cooked tomatillos in blender container or food processor bowl with metal blade; process with on-off pulses just until smooth. Just before serving, in medium bowl combine tomatillos with remaining ingredients.

Red Pepper Corn Relish
Ingredients:
1 medium can red pimientos
1/4 cup water
2 each diced red peppers
2 each diced yellow peppers
1 medium can kernel corn
4 stalks diced celery
4 ounces tomato juice
1/4 cup Marsala wine
2 tablespoons chicken base
2 teaspoons minced garlic
Pinch sweet basil
Pinch sugar
Pinch white pepper
2 tablespoons olive oil
Dash Tabasco sauce
Directions: Place the pimientos, water, red and yellow peppers, kernel corn, and celery and tomato juice in a blender and use the chopped cycle to blend for 10 seconds. Add the remaining ingredients and blend again until hopped but still chunky. Serve hot or cold.

Caponata
(Italian Appetizer)
Ingredients
1 whole globe eggplant, diced
1 onion, red, coarsely chopped
1 medium green bell pepper, diced
1 ¼ Tbsp. capers
2 cloves of garlic, crushed
1-cup tomato paste
½ tsp. Kalamata olives, pitted and chopped
½ Tbsp. Granulated white sugar

½ tsp. Basalmic vinegar
½ tsp. Oregano
black pepper to taste
Dash of hot sauce
Directions: Sauté the first 5 ingredients in olive oil and large skillet. Sauté stirring frequently for 10 minutes. Till eggplant is tender. Add tomato sauce, and next 5 ingredients: cover, reduce heat, and simmer for 30 minutes, stirring frequently.
Add hot sauce and spices to taste. Serve hot or chill 24 hours and serve cold.

Deep Fried Artichoke Hearts
No family holiday was complete without my mother's deep fried artichoke hearts.
Ingredients
2 cans artichoke hearts, drained
3 eggs
1/4 cup 2% milk
2 cups Italian blend bread crumbs
4 cups salad oil
Directions: Heat salad oil in a 10-inch skillet. Crack eggs into bowl. Add milk and mix well. Dip artichokes in egg mixture and then in bread crumbs Drop into hot oil and fry, turning until golden brown. Drain on paper towels. Serve warm.

Fried Calamari
Ingredients
1/2 to 1 pound calamari sliced into rings, I also use the tentacles
1 cup flour
1 tsp paprika
1 tsp cayenne pepper
Enough vegetable oil to fill bottom of heavy skillet to 1/2".
Directions: Clean calamari and keep chilled.

Mix flour, paprika and cayenne in shallow bowl.
Heat oil to 375 degrees. Toss a handful of calamari with flour, shake off excess. Fry for 3 or 4 minutes or until golden brown. Drain on paper towels and salt to taste. I serve this with a marinara sauce, but I add a little dash of Tabasco to it. My family loves spicy foods.
(Cajun influence)

Stuffed Artichoke Bottoms
Ingredients
Preparation Time: 15 minutes
2 ounces lowfat cream cheese or Neufchatel
2 tablespoons crumbled bleu cheese
1 tablespoon lowfat mayonnaise
12 marinated artichoke bottoms
Paprika for garnish
Directions: In a small bowl, mix together cheeses and mayonnaise. Spoon cheese mixture into artichoke bottoms and garnish with a dusting of paprika. Serve at room temperature.
Makes 1 dozen stuffed artichoke bottoms or 6 servings.

Cheese bread
Ingredients
4 each – 6" sourdough baked bread rounds
3 oz Brie cheese
3 oz Grated Havarti cheese
4 – each roasted garlic gloves
¼ teaspoon crushed red peppers
Splash of olive oil
Splash of Balsamic Vinegar
Directions: Cut sourdough round in squares

Take out very little bread and stuff with brie cheese and grated Havarti cheese. Place in oven for 10 minutes until all cheese is melted. Place on plated pour olive oil and balsamic vinegar on plate Garnish with roasted garlic and crushed red peppers.

Easy Spring Rolls
Ingredients
1 pound lean ground beef
1 pound ground pork
1 clove garlic, mashed
1 teaspoon ground ginger
1 large head of cabbage, shredded
1 pound of bean sprouts
1/2 teaspoon Chinese 5 spice
1/4 cup lite soy sauce
1 bunch green onions, chopped
1 package egg roll wrappers
Directions: Brown beef and pork with garlic and ginger. Drain and add cabbage. Sauté until cabbage is tender. Add the bean sprouts, 5 spice, soy sauce and green onions. Mix together well and cook for 1-2 minutes. Drain well. Roll mixture in egg wrappers and deep fry until golden brown. Yield: 48 spring rolls.

Panettone French Toast
Ingredients
Cinnamon Syrup:
1 cup water
1 cup packed dark brown sugar
2 tablespoons whipping cream
1/2 teaspoon ground cinnamon
French Toast:
1 (1.1 pound) loaf panettone bread, baking paper removed
6 large eggs

3/4 cup whipping cream

3/4 cup whole milk (Eggnog maybe be substituted)

1/4 cup sugar

2 tablespoons unsalted butter

1/2 cup mascarpone cheese or Nutella

Powdered sugar, for dusting

Directions

To make the syrup: Combine 1 cup of water and brown sugar in a heavy medium saucepan. Bring to a boil over high heat, stirring until the sugar dissolves. Boil until the syrup reduces to 1 cup, about 10 minutes. Remove from the heat and whisk in the cream and cinnamon. Keep the syrup warm. (The syrup can be made 1 day ahead. Cool, then cover and refrigerate. Rewarm before serving.)

Meanwhile, prepare the French toast: Preheat your flat griddle or large fry pan to 200 degrees F. Trim the bottom crust of the panettone. Starting at the bottom end of the panettone, cut it crosswise into 6 (3/4-inch thick) round slices (reserve the top piece for toast!). In a large bowl, whisk the eggs until well blended. Add the cream, milk, and sugar and whisk until well mixed. Melt 1 tablespoon of butter on a large nonstick griddle over medium heat. Dip 3 slices of panettone into the custard, turning to allow both sides to absorb the custard. Grill the soaked panettone slices until they are golden brown and firm to the touch, about 4 minutes per side. Transfer the French toast to a baking sheet and keep them warm in your oven however I serve as they are ready. Repeat with the remaining butter, panettone slices, and custard.

Transfer the French toast to plates. Dollop the mascarpone and or Nutella atop each. Lightly dust with the powdered sugar. Drizzle the cinnamon syrup over and around the French toast and serve immediately.

Monte Cristo Sandwich

Ingredients

2 eggs

¼ cup of milk

5 tablespoons of softened butter

6 pieces thinly sliced white bread

4 thin slices cooked turkey

1/4 cup milk

5 tablespoons butter, softened

6 pieces thinly sliced white bread

4 thin slices cooked turkey

4 thin slices cooked ham

4 thin slices Swiss cheese

confectioners' sugar, for dusting

red currant jelly, for dipping

Directions

Lightly beat eggs and milk in a shallow bowl. Season with salt and pepper and set aside.

For each sandwich, lightly butter 3 slices of bread on both sides.

Place 2 slices of turkey and 2 of ham between 2 slices of bread.

Top with 2 slices of cheese and add last slice of bread.

Trim crusts, secure with toothpicks, and cut in half on the diagonal.

Melt 2 tablespoons of the butter in a large nonstick skillet over medium heat. Dip sandwich halves, top and bottom, in batter.

When butter foams, place sandwiches in skillet and fry until golden brown, about 2 minutes. Add remaining 2 tablespoons butter to skillet, turn sandwiches, and fry for 2 minutes more.

Transfer to plates, sprinkle with confectioners' sugar, and serve with jelly

Mediterranean Brunch Braid
Ingredients:
1/4 cup extra virgin olive oil
1 1/2 cups chopped green onions (about 24 small)
2 cloves garlic, finely chopped
1 box (9 oz) frozen chopped spinach, thawed, squeezed to drain
1/2 teaspoon salt
1/4 teaspoon pepper
1/4 cup chopped fresh basil leaves
1 cup part-skim ricotta cheese
1/4 cup crumbled feta cheese (1 oz)
2 tablespoons Pine Nuts, toasted*
1 can (13.8 oz) refrigerated pre made classic pizza crust
1 1/2 cups shredded Italian five-cheese blend (6 oz)
4 plum (Roma) tomatoes, thinly sliced
Fresh basil sprigs, if desired
Directions:
Heat oven to 425°F. Spray large cookie sheet with No-Stick Cooking Spray.
In 10-inch skillet, heat 1 tablespoon of the oil over medium heat. Add onions and garlic; cook about 5 minutes, stirring occasionally, until onions are tender. Stir in spinach, salt, pepper and chopped basil. Cook 5 minutes, stirring occasionally. Remove skillet from heat;setaside.In small bowl, mix ricotta cheese, feta cheese and pine nuts; set aside. Unroll pizza crust dough on cookie sheet. Starting at center, press out dough into 15x10-inch rectangle. Brush 1 tablespoon oil over dough. Sprinkle 1/2 cup of the Italian cheese in 5-inch-wide strip lengthwise down center of dough. Spoon spinach mixture over cheese. Spread ricotta mixture over spinach. Layer tomato slices, overlapping, on ricotta mixture. Drizzle 1 tablespoon oil over tomatoes. Sprinkle with 1/2 cup Italian cheese.
Using kitchen scissors or sharp knife, make cuts 1 inch apart on each long side of rectangle to within 1/2 inch of filling. Fold strips of dough

diagonally over filling, alternating from side to side. Turn ends under; press to seal. Brush remaining 1 tablespoon oil over top of braid. Bake 18 to 23 minutes or until crust is deep golden brown. Remove from oven. Sprinkle remaining 1/2 cup Italian cheese over top of braid. Bake about 1 minute longer or until cheese is melted. Let stand 10 minutes. Remove from cookie sheet to cutting board; cut crosswise into slices. Garnish with basil sprigs.

*To toast pine nuts, cook in ungreased heavy skillet over medium heat 5 to 7 minutes, stirring frequently until nuts begin to brown, then stirring constantly until light brown. Remove from skillet to plate to cool.

Pork Filled Wonton
Ingredients
1 package wonton noodles
1 pound pork sausage
4 tablespoons Tamari (soy) sauce
3 teaspoons minced onions
2 cups salad oil
Directions: Combine sausage, Tamari sauce and minced onions. Spoon 1/2 teaspoon of mixture into center of wonton noodle. Fold each noodle in half to form a triangle with filling inside. Dip fingers into cold water, moisten noodle edges and press around the edges to seal in the

filling.

Heat oil in wok to approximately 360 degrees. Drop wonton in oil, cook, stirring for one minute or until golden brown. Lift out with slotted spoon and drain on paper towels. Serve hot.

Ingredients

2   6 ½ ounce crab meat, minced
1 tablespoon snipped chives
3 tablespoons crab base
2 tablespoons lemon juice
1   8 ounce package cream cheese, softened
½ teaspoon Worcestershire sauce

Directions: Combine all ingredients, mixing well. Shape into a large crab shape and chill. Serve with crackers.

Cucumber Dill Yogurt Dip

Ingredients

Three cucumbers peeled and seeded, and put them in the Cuisinart
1 tablespoon of powdered garlic into the Cuisinart
1 teaspoon of salt into the Cuisinart
1 teaspoon white pepper into the Cuisinart
2 tablespoons apple cider vinegar into Cuisinart
2 tablespoons dry dill into Cuisinart.

Directions: Mix the ingredients until cucumbers are completely chopped add the mixture to 1 quart of plain yogurt and stir in a separate bowl.

French Fried Cauliflower

Ingredients

2 pounds cauliflower
1 pound flour
2 eggs
1 tablespoon salt
8 ounces 2% milk   2 cups canola oil

Directions: Clean cauliflower and cut into florets. Blanch for 3-5 minutes and drain. Make a batter using the flour, eggs, salt and milk. Dip dry florets into batter and drain excess batter. Heat oil in deep skillet and fry florets until golden brown. Drain on paper towels. Serve hot.

Spinach Dip
Ingredients
1 cup mayonnaise
1-1/2 cups sour cream
1-10 ounce package frozen, chopped spinach, thawed and drained
1-1.4 ounce package Knorr vegetable or leek soup mix
1- 8 ounce can water chestnuts, drained and chopped
3 green onions, chopped
Directions: Place all ingredients into a mixing bowl and stir until well blended. Cover and chill.
Yield: 4-1/2 cups

Olive Tapenade
Ingredients
1 cup pitted black olives
1 cup pitted green olives
1 cup pitted kalamata olives
1 tablespoon capers
2 cloves garlic, peeled
3 tablespoons balsamic vinegar
3 tablespoons extra virgin olive oil
Directions: Combine the black olives, green olives, kalamata olives, capers and garlic in the container of a food processor. Pulse to chop, and then add balsamic vinegar and olive oil. Process until smooth. Refrigerate for at least one hour, or overnight if possible, before serving. Serve on your best Muffalata sandwich or on a crostini.

Cheese Fondue
Ingredients
Hot Cheese Fondue
1 pound Velveeta Cheese
2 small cans of diced Ortega chilies
1 12 oz can of Italian style stewed tomatoes
1 can (12 oz) beer
1 clove of minced garlic
Directions: Pour beer into slow cooker or double broiler, add block of Velveeta Cheese, cover and simmer till cheese is melted. Add Ortega chilies, Italian style stewed tomatoes and garlic. Stir continually until cheese is melted completely, transfer into your favorite Fondue bowl. Serve with fresh vegetables, corn chips, tortilla chips or cubed sour dough bread.

Stuffed Cherry Tomatoes
Ingredients
10 each cherry tomatoes, washed and dried
3 tablespoons Dijon mustard
1/4 teaspoon lemon juice
1   8 ounce package creamed cheese
1 cup diced shrimp meat
Directions: Cut top of tomatoes off and save caps. Mix all other ingredients together. Put mixture into a pastry bag and using a large tip, pipe mixture inside of tomatoes. Place caps on top. Cover and chill. Yield: 10 servings

Cranberry Chutney
Ingredients
1 C. water
4 C. fresh cranberries
1 C. raisins
2 C. sugar
1/2 t. ginger
1 t. cinnamon
1/2 t. allspice
1/2 t. salt
1 (8 oz.) can crushed pineapple, drained (add juice to water to make 1 cup)
Directions: Mix all the ingredients together, except for the pineapple and raisins. Mix well. Cook over medium heat until the cranberries begin to pop. Add the pineapple and raisins. Cook for another 20 minutes, until mixture thickens. Refrigerate for up to 2 weeks.

Spinach frittata
Ingredients
1 teaspoon olive oil
1 garlic clove, minced
3 cups baby spinach leaves
3 whole eggs, plus 4 egg whites
1/2 yellow onion, chopped
1/4 cup minced red bell pepper
2 tablespoons chopped fresh basil
1/4 cup shredded part-skim mozzarella or provolone cheese
¼ teaspoons of seasoning salt
Directions
Preheat the broiler. Position the rack 4 inches from the heat source. In a large, nonstick frying pan with a flameproof handle, heat 1/2 teaspoon of the olive oil over medium heat. Add the garlic and saute until softened, about 1 minute. Stir in the spinach and cook until it

wilts, 1 to 2 minutes. Transfer to a bowl. Set the frying pan aside.
In a bowl, whisk together the whole eggs and egg whites. Add the
seasoning salt. Set aside.
Return the frying pan to medium heat and heat the remaining 1/2
teaspoon olive oil. Add the onion and saute until soft and translucent,
about 4 minutes. Stir in the remaining 1/2 teaspoon salt, the bell
pepper and the potatoes and cook until the potatoes begin to brown
but are still tender-crisp, 4 to 5 minutes.
Spread the spinach evenly over the bottom of the pan. Sprinkle with
the basil. Pour in the beaten eggs and sprinkle evenly with the cheese.
Cook until slightly set, about 2 to 3 minutes.
Carefully place the pan under the broiler and broil until the frittata is
brown and puffy and completely set, about 3 minutes. Gently slide
onto a warmed serving platter and cut into wedges. Serve
immediately. Serves 4

Aegean Salad
Ingredients
½ cup Greek olives
4 cups red leaf lettuce torn
4 cups green leaf lettuce torn
½ cup red onion slivered
1 medium tomato chopped
½ cup feta cheese crumbled
--Oregano Dressing—
1 tablespoon red wine vinegar
2 teaspoons lemon juice
1 clove garlic minced
½ teaspoon salt
½ teaspoon dried oregano
1/8 teaspoon ground pepper
¼ cup olive oil
Directions: In a small bowl combine dressing with olives; cover and let stand for 30 minutes at room temperature. In a small bowl combine lettuce onion, tomato, and green pepper. Mix lightly with olives and Oregano Dressing. Sprinkle with cheese. Oregano Dressing: In a small bowl mix vinegar, lemon juice, garlic, salt, oregano, and pepper. Using a whisk or fork, gradually beat in oil until well blended. Makes about 1/3 cup.

Baby Asparagus Salad
Ingredients
1 cup mayonnaise
1 teaspoon Dijon mustard
1 tablespoon white wine vinegar
1 pound baby asparagus
1 cup medium size shrimp, cooked, with tail on.
Cherry tomatoes

Melba toast
1 cup sour cream
1 can golden caviar
Directions: Mix mayonnaise with mustard and vinegar and set aside. Gently peel stalk of asparagus. In a 12-inch frying pan, lay spears parallel, in boiling water to cover. Boil until easily pierced, drain at once. Plunge the hot spears into a bowl of ice water. When cool, drain and chill. Arrange 6 chilled and drained spears on a plate. Place 3 shrimp on top. Put 2 pieces of melba toast on plate with sour cream and caviar. Place 2 tablespoons of mayonnaise mixture next to asparagus.

Caesar Salad
Ingredients
1 head romaine lettuce
1 cup Parmesan cheese
1 cup croutons
Dressing
2 eggs
3 teaspoons Worcestershire sauce
2 tablespoons olive oil
1 teaspoon crushed garlic
3 anchovies, chopped very fine
Prepare dressing: Beat eggs in mixing bowl, and add olive oil, garlic, Worcestershire sauce and diced anchovies. Mix very well and chill. Chop romaine lettuce and add cheese, croutons and dressing. Serve immediately.

Caprese Salad
Ingredients
2 large red or yellow tomatoes, sliced
1/2 pound fresh Mozzarella cheese, drained, sliced
1 bunch fresh basil leaves
3 tablespoons Extra Virgin olive oil
1 tablespoons balsamic vinegar
salt and freshly ground black pepper
Directions: Arrange tomato, cheese slices and basil alternately
overlapping on platter.
Whisk oil and vinegar together. Pour over tomatoes. Season to taste
with salt and pepper.

Carrot Salad
Ingredients
1 bunch grated carrots
1/3 cup raisins
1/3 cup crushed pineapple, with juice
1 cup mayonnaise
3/4 cup diced celery
1/4 cup diced red onion
Salt and black pepper to taste
Directions: In a large bowl add carrots, raisins, pineapple with juice,
mayonnaise, celery and onions. Add salt and pepper to taste and toss
well. Chill thoroughly. Yield: 10 servings

Cole Slaw
Ingredients
1-1/2 cups mayonnaise
1/4 cup milk
2 teaspoons white pepper
1/4 cup red wine vinegar
1 head chopped or finely grated cabbage
2 cups chopped or finely grated carrots
1 small diced green bell pepper
Directions: In a small bowl, mix together well the mayonnaise, milk, white pepper and vinegar to make the dressing. In a large bowl, mix together the cabbage, carrots and bell peppers. Add the dressing and toss well. Cover and refrigerate for 2 hours. Serve cold.

Chicken Raspberry Salad
This is a great salad for dinner.
Ingredients
¼ cup-sugar free raspberry jam
3 t. extra virgin olive oil
¼ cup red wine vinegar
¾ pound boneless cooked chicken breast, cut into strips
6 cups of mixed greens (I prefer mesclun mix)
2 cups fresh cleaned raspberries
½ cup sliced walnuts
Directions: In a resalable jar, combine the jam, oil and vinegar. Close the lid tightly and shake until blended. In a large bowl, tossed the cooked chicken with the dressing. In a large serving bowl add the mesclun mix (rinse with cool water prior to adding into bowl). Top with the chicken mixture, raspberries, and walnuts. Makes 4 serving.

Creole Green Bean Salad
Ingredients
1 package (16 ounces) frozen cut green beans
5 bacon strips, diced
1 medium onion, chopped
1/2 cup chopped green pepper
2 tablespoons all-purpose flour
2 tablespoons brown sugar
1 tablespoon Worcestershire sauce
1 teaspoon salt
1/2 teaspoon pepper
1/2 teaspoon ground mustard
1 can (14-1/2 ounces) diced tomatoes, undrained
Directions
Cook beans according to package directions. Meanwhile, in a skillet, cook bacon, onion and green pepper over medium heat until bacon is crisp and vegetables are tender. Remove with a slotted spoon.
Stir the flour, brown sugar, Worcestershire sauce, salt, pepper and mustard into the drippings until blended. Stir in tomatoes. Bring to a boil; cook and stir for 2 minutes or until thickened. Drain beans and add to skillet. Stir in bacon mixture. Yield: 6 servings.

Greek Salad
Ingredients
3 cups lettuce mixed with the Italian herb vinaigrette
8 pieces of bell pepper cut into circles
6 pieces of red onion cut into circles
4pieces of Salami cut into rectangle strips
½ cup Kalamata pitted olives, chopped
1/4 cup of Feta Cheese
Directions: Place lettuce in bowl, add rest of ingredients and a handful of feta cheese sprinkled on top of salami.

Grilled Spicy Filet Mignon Salad with Ginger Lime Dressing
Ingredients
3 tablespoons soy sauce
1 tablespoon fresh lime juice
1 tablespoon chili paste with garlic
1 tablespoon peanut oil
2 (12-ounce) filet mignons
Freshly ground pepper

Directions
Whisk soy sauce, lime juice, chile paste, and peanut oil together in a small baking dish. Add the steaks, turn to coat, cover, and let marinate for 30 minutes in the refrigerator. Remove from the refrigerator 15 minutes before grilling.
Heat grill to high. Remove steaks from marinade and pat dry. Season both sides with pepper and grill for 3 minutes per side or until slightly charred and cooked to medium-rare doneness. Remove from the grill, let rest 5 minutes, and slice into 1/4-inch thick slices.

Salad:
1 head Bibb lettuce, torn into bite-size pieces
3 cups mizuna leaves, torn into bite-size pieces
1/4 cup chiffonade Thai basil or regular basil, optional
1/2 English cucumber, halved and cut crosswise into 1/4-inch thick slices
2 carrots, julienned
5 radishes, thinly sliced
8 each yellow and red cherry tomatoes, halved
Ginger Lime Dressing, recipe follows
Salt and ground black pepper
While steak is resting, combine all salad ingredients in a large bowl. Toss with half of the dressing and season with salt and pepper. Transfer to a platter, top with the steak, and drizzle the remaining dressing over the top.

Ginger-Lime Dressing:
1/4 cup fresh lime juice
1 tablespoon soy sauce
1 tablespoon rice vinegar
1 tablespoon finely diced shallot
1 tablespoon finely grated fresh ginger
2 teaspoons sugar
2 tablespoons peanut oil
Salt and freshly ground pepper
Whisk ingredients together in a small bowl. Season with salt and pepper, to taste. Let sit 10 minutes before using. Serves: 4 servings

Macaroni Salad
This was one of my dad's favorite recipes
Ingredients
4 cups cooked macaroni
1 cup finely chopped celery
1/4 finely chopped red onion
1 4 ounce can finely chopped pimiento
4 finely chopped hard boiled eggs
1/3 cup pickle relish
1 small can chopped olives
1 tablespoon dry mustard
1-1/2 cups mayonnaise
1/4 teaspoon salt
Dash of white pepper
1 teaspoon Salad Supreme seasoning
Directions: Place all ingredients into a large bowl and toss to mix well. Cover and refrigerate before serving. Serve very cold. (Note: Always make the day ahead of use. If "tight" after standing all night, loosen with milk ~ very little will work.) Yield: 6 servings

Mediterranean Salad

Ingredients
3 tablespoons extra-virgin olive oil, plus 1/4 cup
2 cloves garlic, minced
1 (1-pound) box Israeli couscous (or any small pasta)
3 cups vegetable stock
2 lemons, juiced
1 lemon, zested
1/2 teaspoon salt
1/2 teaspoon freshly ground black pepper
1 cup chopped fresh basil leaves
1/2 cup chopped fresh mint leaves
1/4 cup dried cranberries
1/4 cup slivered almonds, toasted

Directions
In a medium saucepan, warm 3 tablespoons of the olive oil over medium heat. Add the garlic and cook for 1 minute. Add the couscous and cook until toasted and lightly browned, stirring often, about 5 minutes. Carefully add the stock, and the juice of 1 lemon, and bring to a boil. Reduce the heat and simmer, covered, until the couscous is tender, but still firm to the bite, stirring occasionally, about 8 to 10 minutes. Drain the couscous.
In a large bowl, toss the cooked couscous with the remaining olive oil, remaining lemon juice, zest, salt, and pepper and let cool.
Once the couscous is room temperature, add the fresh herbs, dried cranberries, and almonds. Toss to combine and serve.

Marinated Carrot Salad
Ingredients
1 medium can sliced carrots
1/4 cup red onion, sliced thin
2 celery stalks, chopped

1 cup Italian dressing
1/2 teaspoon oregano
1/3 teaspoon sweet basil
Directions: Drain carrots and place in bowl. Add onion and celery and mix together. Add oregano and sweet basil to bottled dressing and mix together well. Add dressing to salad. Store in refrigerator for 12 - 14 hours. Yield: 8 servings

Crispy Parmesan Bowls
Serves: 8 servings
Ingredients
2 cups grated Parmesan
8 cups prepared Caesar salad, for serving
Directions:
In a large nonstick skillet, spread 1/4 cup cheese thinly and evenly over the bottom to form a 7-inch circle. Put the pan over medium heat and cook until the cheese is bubbling and lightly browned, about 3 minutes. Remove the pan from the heat. Put a small bowl upside down on a cutting board. When the bubbling stops, about 1 minute, carefully remove the disk with a thin metal spatula and drape it over the bowl. Press gently with the spatula so it forms a bowl. Be careful, as it is very fragile. Let cool.
Remove the Parmesan bowl, put it onto a plate, and fill with Caesar salad. Serve

Orange and Grape Salad
Ingredients
3 large navel oranges, sliced thin
2 bunches red seedless grapes, washed and drained
1 bunch butter lettuce, cleaned and drained
Mint leaves
Dressing
1/4 cucumber, finely chopped or grated

Salt and pepper to taste
1 tablespoon olive oil
1 teaspoon white vinegar
1 tablespoon crushed garlic
1/2 cup plain yogurt
2 tablespoons chopped fresh mint
Directions: Mix all dressing ingredients together. Chill until served. Place lettuce liner on each plate. Place two large orange slices (or three medium), on lettuce. Place grapes next to oranges and add two tablespoons of dressing on top of the oranges. Garnish with whole mint leaves. Yield: 4 servings

Orange Salad
(Insalata d'Arance)
This typically Sicilian salad is excellent as a side dish, or a separate course leading into dessert. Serves 6
Ingredients
4 large navel oranges,
1 large fresh anise bulb (the crisper the better),
1 small lemon,
1/4 cup shelled almonds,
1 tablespoon extra-virgin olive oil,
1 tablespoon white sugar,
1 tablespoon sweet Marsala wine,
1 head of lettuce,
Directions: Dried coconut shavings, a branch of fresh peppermint leaves. Preparation: Separate mint leaves from stalk. Clean the anise well. Peel the oranges and lemon, and remove the tough heart of the anise, as well as the stalk and leaves. Cut the anise, oranges and lemon crosswise into thin slices. Toss together with almonds and mint leaves in a large bowl. Sprinkle with sugar, olive oil and Marsala wine, and toss again. Chill for a few hours. Toss again before serving. Serve on a bed of lettuce leaves. Sprinkle dried coconut shavings over the top.

Potato Salad

My dad used this salad at all of his catered functions ~ it was always a hit

Ingredients

8 potatoes

1 teaspoon chopped dried parsley

1 package Hidden Valley Original dressing (dry)

4 coarsely chopped hard cooked eggs

1/4 cup diced red onion

1 teaspoon Salad Supreme seasoning

1 tablespoon dry mustard

1 small can chopped olives

1-1/2 cups mayonnaise

4 tablespoons lemon juice

1/2 teaspoon white pepper

1/4 teaspoon salt

2 finely chopped celery nibs

Directions: Preheat oven to 400 F. Wash potatoes thoroughly and dry. Wrap in foil and bake for 1-1/2 hours. Remove and cool in foil in refrigerator over night. Peel and cut potatoes into small pieces. Place all ingredients into a large bowl and gently fold until all pieces are well coated. If potatoes seem a little dry, add more mayonnaise. The salad is best if made 1 or 2 days ahead. Always cover salad when stored in refrigerator. (Note: If you prefer a salad with reduced fat, use a fat-free mayonnaise.) Yield: 6 servings

Shanghai Chicken Salad
Ingredients
4 each tender, moist chicken breast halves, boneless and skinless
2 heads fresh lettuce
Crisp rice noodles
1/2 cup toasted almond halves
1/4 cup chopped green onions
1/4 cup mandarin orange slices
Dressing
1/4 cup soy sauce
2 cups salad oil
1/2 cup rice vinegar
2 tablespoons sesame seeds
1/4 cup sesame oil
Directions: Combine all ingredients for dressing, mix well and chill. In a large bowl, place chopped lettuce, cooked, diced chicken breasts, almonds, onions and oranges and toss gently. Add dressing and toss. Place on plate and surround with cooked rice noodles. Yield: 16 servings

Three Bean Salad
Ingredients
2 - 16 ounce cans cut green beans
2 - 16 ounce cans garbanzo beans
2 - 16 ounce cans large red kidney beans
3 cups bite-sized pieces of celery
1 medium diced red onion
8 ounces bottled Italian salad dressing
Directions: Open all cans and drain. In a large bowl add all items and mix well. Cover and refrigerate for 30 minutes before serving. Yield: 10 servings

Tuna or Chicken Salad
Ingredients
4 cups bite-sized cooked chicken pieces
1 cup chopped celery
1/8 cup finely chopped red onion
2 finely chopped hard cooked eggs
1/2 cup mayonnaise
1/4 cup pickle relish
1/2 cup sour cream
2 teaspoons Salad Supreme seasoning
1/4 teaspoon salt
1/8 teaspoon white pepper
Directions: Place chicken in bowl and add celery, onions and eggs.
Combine mayonnaise, relish and sour cream and blend well. Add Salad
Supreme seasoning and salt and pepper and mix well. Toss with
chicken until well mixed. (Note: For tuna salad replaces the chicken
pieces with 1-1/2 cups water-packed, drained, flaked tuna. Also add 3
tablespoons of lemon juice to mayonnaise mixture. Yield: 4 servings

Taco Salad
Ingredients
Doritos Chips or Frito's
1 pound hamburger
3 cups finely shredded lettuce
1 cup chopped black olives
3 cups chopped fine tomatoes
1 cup diced red onion
3 cups shredded Mexican cheese
1 cup of Catalina Dressing or French dressing
¼ cup of Pico Pico Sauce if desired

Directions: Slowly cook hamburger in skillet being careful not to brown. Break into small pieces and drain all fat from pan. Place into shallow pan and refrigerate for ½ hour. In large bowl add the chopped lettuce, cooked chilled hamburger, olives, tomatoes', onions, and cheese. Mix well. Add dressing and salsa. Mix well. Take the chips and break them up, add to salad just prior to serving. Enjoy....

Spinach Dijon Salad
Ingredients
2 bunches fresh spinach
1/2 cup diced red tomatoes
1/4 cup cooked diced bacon
1/4 cup cooked diced hardboiled egg
Combine dressing ingredients and mix well.
Directions: Clean spinach very well and rinse well. Chop into bite size pieces. Place into individual serving bowls and top with tomatoes, bacon and egg. Add dressing (approximately 1/4 cup per salad). Yield: 6 - 8 servings

Dijon Dressing
Ingredients
2 cups honey
1/2 cup Dijon mustard
Directions: In mixing bowl, mix the two ingredients together till well blended and 2 oz over stalad.

Oriental Salad
Ingredients
1 cup salad oil
1/4 cup rice vinegar
1/3 cup sesame seed oil
3 tablespoons soy sauce
1/3 cup sesame seeds

1 egg, beaten
1/2 cup rice noodles
64 mandarin orange wedges
1 head chopped iceberg lettuce
Directions: Combine oil, vinegar, sesame seed oil, soy sauce, sesame seeds and egg, and mix very well. Add dressing to chopped lettuce on plate. Top with mandarin orange wedges and surround with rice noodles. Yield: 8 servings

Sicilian Dressing
Ingredients
3 ounces vinegar
4 ounces sugar
6 ounces salad oil
1 small teaspoon paprika
1/3 teaspoon dry mustard
1/2 teaspoon salt
1/2 teaspoon minced onion
1/3 teaspoon celery seed
Directions: In a small sauce pan, heat vinegar and sugar until sugar is thoroughly dissolved. Add remaining ingredients. Let stand 24 hours before serving. Yield: 12 servings

Soups

Albondigas Soup
MEATBALLS (ALBONDIGAS) :
1/2 c. bread or cracker crumbs
1/4 c. milk
1 egg
1/2 lb. each ground beef and ground pork
Salt and pepper
1/4 c. minced onion
2 cloves garlic, minced
1 tbsp. fresh mint, minced or 2 tsp. dried
Mix together and shape into small balls. Brown lightly on all sides.
SOUP:
1 tbsp. oil
1 sm. onion, chopped
1 clove garlic, minced
5 c. water or chicken broth
4 chicken bouillon cubes (if no broth)
1/2 (8 oz.) can tomato sauce
1 carrot, sliced

1 zucchini, sliced
2 tomatoes, chopped
Heat oil in large pan. Cook onion and garlic until soft. Stir in broth and tomato sauce. Simmer 10 minutes. Add meatballs and carrots. Simmer 20 minutes. Add zucchini and tomatoes. Simmer 10 minutes.

Butternut Squash Bisque Recipe
Ingredients
1/4 cup chopped shallots
1/4 cup chopped celery
1/4 cup chopped carrots
1/2 tsp. Allspice
Salt and White pepper
1/4 cup vegetable oil
2 cups water
2 cups heavy cream
Directions: Preheat Oven to 350. Wash and stem squash. Cut butternut squash lengthwise. On large sheet tray with at least 1" sides, place squash cut side down. Rub with oil and add water (to help cook). Cook for 30-40 minutes. Cool, then scoop out the meat from inside. In a 2 quart non-stick pan cook celery, shallot, and carrots in 2 T butter until soft, 3-5 minutes.
Add all squash and seasonings. Using a food processor blend squash until smooth. Add cream, salt, pepper, and nutmeg to taste. Heat on low stirring constantly.

Simply Put
I Love
Being A Chef

Cioppino

Ingredients
1/4 cup olive oil
1 Tbsp chopped garlic
1 Tbsp chopped flat-leaf parsley
1/2 cup chopped celery
1/2 cup chopped green pepper
1 small onion, chopped
1 chopped jalapeno pepper (optional)
3 cups solid pack tomatoes
1 cup tomato sauce
1 Tbsp fresh basil or 1 tsp dried basil
1 Tbsp Cajun Seasoning salt
1 Tsp freshly ground black pepper
1 Tbsp paprika
1/2 cup dry sherry wine
1/2 cup dry Marsala wine
2 1/2 cups water
1 lb white fish chopped (tilapia, catfish, swordfish)
1 lb scallops small.
1 lb shrimp
Optional: Mussels, Clams, Calamari, Octopus, etc.
Optional: 1 lemon cut into wedges

Directions

In a large pot, saute onion, green pepper, celery, and jalapeno pepper in olive oil for 5 minutes. Add garlic, and parsley and saute for an additional 2 minutes. Add tomatoes, tomato sauce, salt, black pepper, paprika, and sherry. Cook for 15 minutes. Add white and red wine and water, and cook on low heat for 1 hour uncovered. This can all be completed hours before serving.

When ready to serve, add fish and shellfish, cover, and cook for 6-8 minutes until fish is just cooked through.

Serve piping hot with crusty Italian bread and lemon wedges if desired.

Carrot and Orange Soup

Ingredients

2 tablespoons butter

1 pound carrots, thinly sliced

1 large onion, sliced

3 cups chicken broth, regular strength

1 teaspoon sugar

1/2 teaspoon dill weed

1-1/2 cups fresh orange juice

Salt to taste

Directions: Melt butter in a 5 - 6 quart pan. Add carrots and onions. Cook, stirring until onion is limp. Add chicken broth, sugar and dill weed. Cover and simmer 35 minutes or until carrots are very tender when pierced. Start with half of the mixture and blend, adding the rest of the mixture and blending until smooth. Stir in the orange juice. Cover and chill. Season to taste with salt. Serve chilled or reheat just to simmering.

Chicken Tortilla Soup
Ingredients
1 tablespoon plus 1 teaspoon extra virgin olive oil
2 ½ cups chopped onion
2 tablespoons chopped garlic
2 (6-inch) corn tortillas, chopped
2 tablespoons tomato paste
4 teaspoons Mexican or Cajun seasoning
6 cups reduced-sodium chicken broth
1 (15 oz) can diced tomatoes
1 (14 oz) can yellow hominy, drained and rinsed
1 (14 oz) can black beans, drained and rinsed
2 cups cooked chopped chicken
Juice of one lime
Topping
1 ¼ cups reduced-fat tortilla chips, crushed
Directions
In a large nonstick pot, add the olive oil, onions and garlic. Saute for 1 minute.
Add the chopped tortillas, tomato paste, and seasonings and saute for 2 minutes. Stir in the chicken broth and tomatoes. Bring up to a boil, turn down heat and simmer for 15 minutes. Add the hominy, beans and chicken and mix well. Simmer for 10 more minutes.

Italian Wedding Soup
Ingredients
1/2 lb lean ground beef
1 egg, slightly beaten
2 tablespoons breadcrumbs
1 tablespoon parmesan cheese
1/2 teaspoon dried basil
1/2 teaspoon onion powder
5 3/4 cups chicken broth

2 cups chopped escarole or 2 cups chopped spinach
1/2 cup orzo pasta, uncooked
1/3 cup finely chopped carrot
grated parmesan cheese
Directions: In medium bowl combine, meat, egg,bread crumbs,
parmesan cheese, basil& onion powder; shape into 3/4" balls.
In large sauce pan, heat broth to boiling; stir in spinach, orzo, carrot&
meatballs. Return to boil; reduce heat to medium.
Cook at slow boil for 10 minutes or until orzo is tender.
Stir frequently to avoid sticking. Serve with additional Parmesan
cheese sprinkled on top

Minestrone
Servings: 8 to 10
Ingredients:
3 garlic cloves
3 large onions
2 celery sticks
2 large carrots
3 1/2 ounces zucchini
4 tbsp butter
1/2 cup olive oil
7 cups vegetable or chicken stock
1 bunch fresh basil, finely chopped
1 tsp dried oregano
3 1/2 ounces chopped tomatoes
2 tbsp tomato paste
3 1/2 ounces Parmesan cheese rind
3 ounces small shell Pasta
salt and pepper
freshly grated Parmesan cheese, to serve
Directions: Finely chop the garlic, onions, celery, carrots, and zucchini
using a sharp knife. Heat the butter and oil together in a large

saucepan, add the garlic and onion and fry for 2 minutes, then stir in the celery, carrots, and fry for minutes longer, stirring the vegetables occasionally. Add the beans to the saucepan and fry for 2 minutes. Stir in the zucchini and cook for 2 minutes longer. Cover and cook all the vegetables, stirring frequently, for about 15 minutes.

Add the stock, basil, oregano, tomatoes, tomato paste, and cheese rind and season to taste. Bring to a boil, lower the heat and simmer for 1 hour. Remove and discard the cheese rind. Add the shell pasta to the pan and cook for 20 minutes. Serve sprinkled with freshly grated Parmesan cheese on top.

Oxtail Soup
5 lbs oxtails (meaty)
kosher salt
black pepper
14 cup all-purpose flour
2 tbsps olive oil
1 onion (chopped)
2 carrots (cut into half moons about 14 inch thick)
2 stalks celery (cut into 14-inch thick pieces)
3 tbsps dried basil
2 tbsps dried oregano
4 cloves cloves garlic (peeled and smashed)
14 cup water
4 cups Marsala wine (dry)
2 cups beef broth
2 bay leaves
12 ozs egg noodles (wide)
4 tbsps unsalted butter (divided)
1 shallot (finely diced)
2 cloves cloves garlic (finely diced)
kosher salt
black pepper

2 tbsps chives (minced)

2 tbsps parmesan (grated)

Directions: Wash and dry the oxtails. Add the meat to a large bowl and season with salt and pepper, to taste. Toss the meat in the flour until lightly coated.

Add the olive oil to a large Dutch oven over medium heat. Brown the oxtails on all sides, in batches, until well browned. Transfer the meat to a plate and pour off some of the drippings, if necessary.

Add the onions, carrots, celery, basil, oregano, and garlic to the pot and sauté until the onions are tender and beginning to brown, about 5 minutes. Season with salt and pepper, to taste. Stir in the Marsala wine. Deglaze the pot with the wine and stir up all the browned bits on the bottom of the pan. Stir in the beef broth, and the bay leaves. Add the shallot and garlic

Add the browned beef back into the pot along with any accumulated juices that may have collected on the plate. Bring the stew to a boil, and then reduce the heat to a low simmer. Cover and cook until the beef is tender and falling off the bone, about 3 1/2 hours.

Cook uncovered, for 30 minutes more. Taste for seasoning. Add salt and pepper, if needed. Add the Buttered noodles. Stir in the chives. After Buttered noodles are firm and cooked transfer to serving bowl garnish with Parmesan cheese.

Peanut Butter Soup

Sounds really different, but it's absolutely wonderful! 4 servings

Ingredients

2 medium onions, chopped

2 tablespoons butter

1 tablespoon flour

2 cups chicken broth

1/2 cup 2% milk

2-1/2 cups creamy peanut butter

Salt to taste

Freshly ground pepper to taste
Whipped cream (optional)
Dash nutmeg
Directions: Sauté onions in butter in large sauce pan over low heat until onions are soft. Sprinkle in flour, stir and cook 2-3 minutes. Gradually add broth and milk, whisking thoroughly. Add peanut butter and cook gently for 15 minutes. Add salt and pepper to taste. Pour into bowls and add a dollop of whipped cream dusted with nutmeg.

Pumpkin Soup
Ingredients
2 medium onions, chopped
2 tablespoons butter
1 tablespoon flour
3 cups chicken broth
3 cups pumpkin puree
Salt to taste
Freshly ground pepper to taste
1/2 cup cream, whipped
Dash nutmeg
Directions: Sauté the onions in butter in a heavy, large sauce pan over low heat until the onions are soft. Sprinkle in the flour, stir and cook for 2 or 3 minutes. Gradually add the chicken broth, whisking thoroughly. Next add the pumpkin puree and cook gently for about 15 minutes. Add salt and pepper to taste. Pour into warm bowls and top with a dollop of whipped cream and a dusting of nutmeg.   Yield: 6 - 8 servings

Vichyssoise
Ingredients
4 tablespoons butter
1 chopped white onion
4 leeks finely chopped (white part only)
2 chopped celery stalks
2 peeled and sliced medium potatoes
2 sprigs fresh parsley
4 cups chicken stock or canned broth
1 cup heavy cream
1 tablespoon finely chopped chives
Salt and freshly ground black pepper to taste
Directions: Melt the butter in a large pot. Add the onions, leeks and celery and cook over low heat, stirring often, for 10-15 minutes or until limp but not brown. Stir in the potatoes, parsley and stock. Cook partially covered until the potatoes are tender ~ about 20 minutes. Put through a strainer or vegetable mill or puree in a blender or food processor. Pour into a bowl, stir in the cream and chives and chill in the refrigerator. Add salt and pepper to taste before serving. Yield: 4 servings.

Shrimp Bisque

Ingredients
1 1/2 pounds shrimp, shelled and deveined, shells reserved
Extra-virgin olive oil
1 stick (8 tablespoons) unsalted butter
2 1eeks, trimmed, halved lengthwise, and rinsed well
3 stalks celery, cut into big chunks
2 carrots, cut into big chunks
3 sprigs fresh thyme
1 bay leaf
2 strips orange zest
2 tablespoons tomato paste

1/4 cup brandy
3 tablespoons all-purpose flour
4 cups heavy cream
Kosher salt and freshly ground black pepper
Finely grated orange zest, for garnish
Finely chopped fresh chives, for garnish

Directions
Heat 3 tablespoons olive oil in a large pot over medium heat and melt the butter into it. Then add the shrimp shells, the leeks, **celery**, carrots, 3 sprigs thyme, the bay leaf, orange zest, and tomato paste. Cook, stirring every now and then, until the shells are red and the vegetables are soft, about 10 minutes.

Take the pot off the heat and carefully pour in the brandy. Ignite the brandy with a long kitchen match and let burn until the flame subsides. Return the pot to the heat, sprinkle in the flour, give it a stir, and cook for another 2 minutes. Now add water to cover and **deglaze**, scraping up all the browned bits on the bottom of the pot with a wooden spoon. Add the cream and bring to a boil. Immediately turn the heat down to low and gently simmer until the soup is reduced and thickened, 30 to 45 minutes. Strain into a clean pot and season with salt and pepper. Chop the shrimp. Return the bisque to a simmer, add the shrimp and cook 2 to 3 minutes just to cook the shrimp through. Give the **bisque** a final taste for seasoning, pour it into warmed soup bowls and serve garnished with the orange zest and chives.

Winter Squash and Apple Soup
Ingredients
2 tablespoons (1/2 stick) unsalted butter
1 medium onion, diced
2 tablespoons peeled and minced fresh ginger
2 medium garlic cloves, pressed
1 - 2-1/2 pound hubbard or butternut squash, peeled, seeded, and cut into 1 inch cubes

1 pound tart green apples (pippin or Granny Smith), peeled, cored and coarsely chopped
4 cups rich chicken stock
1-1/2 cups 2% milk
1/3 cup dry sherry
1-2 tablespoons (to taste) fresh lemon juice
1 tablespoon firmly packed brown sugar
1-1/2 teaspoons salt or to taste
1 teaspoon grated lemon peel
Freshly ground pepper

Directions: Melt butter in a heavy non-aluminum sauce pan over medium heat. Add onion and cook until soft, stirring occasionally (about 8 minutes). Add ginger and garlic and cook until onion begins to color (about 4 minutes).

Add squash and apples and cook for 3 minutes, stirring to prevent sticking. Add stock and bring to a boil. Reduce heat, cover partially and simmer until squash and apples are very tender (about 45 to 60 minutes). Puree soup in batches in a food mill or processor. Return puree to sauce pan. Add milk, sherry, lemon juice, sugar, salt, lemon peel and pepper. Simmer over medium low heat for 25 minutes, stirring frequently. Adjust seasoning, if needed. This recipe can be prepared 1 day ahead and refrigerated. Reheat before serving.

Entrée's
American Recipes

Barbecued Turkey Tenderloin
Ingredients
1 (about 12 ounces) turkey tenderloin, cut into 8 slices
1/2 cup barbecue sauce
1/3 cup finely chopped green bell pepper
3 tablespoons finely chopped red onion
Directions: Place turkey slices in shallow dish or resealable plastic bag. In small bowl, combine barbecue sauce, bell pepper and onion; mix well. Pour over turkey slices in dish. Turn to coat well. Line 15x10x1-inch baking pan with foil; spray foil with nonstick cooking spray. Place turkey slices on foil-lined pan. Broil 4 to 6 inches from heat for 4 minutes. Turn slices; baste with any remaining marinade. Broil an additional 2 to 4 minutes or until turkey is no longer pink and juices run clear.

Beef Stew

Ingredients:

3 LBS Beef Stew Meat, cut into 1-inch cubes
2 Large Onions, sliced
1 CUP Diced Celery
Carrots, bag or cut 1/2-inch thick coins (about the same amount as potatoes)
3 Large Potatoes, in 1-inch cubes
1 TBS minced Garlic
1 TBS Parsley
1 TBS Sweet Basil
3 Large Bay Leaves
1 Quart Better than Bouillon Beef Base made with Water, to taste
1 CUP Red Wine, to taste
Olive Oil (to sauté meat)
Flour (enough to coat meat)
Garlic Powder and Lawry salt (for mixing with Flour)
Pepper, to taste
Lemon Pepper, to taste

Directions:

Sprinkle the beef cubes lightly with Lawry Salt, Garlic Powder, and Flour for extra flavor during browning.

Brown the Floured Beef Cubes in Olive Oil and then sauté Celery and Onions in same fry pan before transferring them to Dutch Oven or Crock-Pot.

Using a Dutch oven heat Beef Base, Wine, Garlic, Parsley, Sweet Basil, and Bay Leaves.

Add Browned Meat, Celery and Onions to Dutch Oven and simmer around 3-4 hours until meat starts to become tender. Then add Carrots and after carrots start to soften around last half hour of cooking add Potatoes and continue to simmer until tender. Add a few tablespoons of flour at the same time to thicken the gravy, or by stirring a tablespoon or so of cornstarch into cold water before adding to the stew. Allow ample time for the thickener to cook before serving time to avoid a raw flour taste.

In a Crock-pot, add all the vegetables at the beginning; set the Crock-Pot to 170-190°F and leave to cook from 5-8 hours or until meat and vegetables are tender. *For the best results Beef Stew made in the Crock-Pot, be sure Crock-Pot doesn't boil; it should simmer lightly. Boiling will make the beef stringy and dry, will ruin the flavor of the broth and make the vegetables mushy.*

Extra vegetables can be added: Turnips, corn, sweet potatoes, fresh peas and green beans.

This stew tastes even better the following day after the flavors have a chance to blend in the refrigerator.

Beef Stroganoff
Ingredients:
6 Tbsp butter
1 pound of top sirloin or tenderloin, cut thin into 1-inch wide by 2 1/2-inch long strips
1/3 cup chopped shallots (can substitute onions)
1/2 pound cremini mushrooms, sliced
Salt to taste
Pepper to taste
1/8 teaspoon nutmeg
1/2 teaspoon of dry tarragon or 2 teaspoons of chopped fresh tarragon
1 cup of sour cream at room temperature
Directions:
Melt 3 Tbsp of butter in a large skillet on medium heat. Increase the

heat to high/med-high and add the strips of beef. You want to cook the beef quickly, browning on each side, so the temp needs to be high enough to brown the beef, but not so high as to burn the butter. You may need to work in batches. While cooking the beef, sprinkle with some salt and pepper. When both sides are browned, remove the beef to a bowl and set aside.

In the same pan, reduce the heat to medium and add the shallots. Cook the shallots for a minute or two, allowing them to soak up any meat drippings. Remove the shallots to the same bowl as the meat and set aside.

In the same pan, melt another 3 Tbsp of butter. Increase heat to medium high and add the mushrooms. Cook, stirring occasionally for about 4 minutes. While cooking, sprinkle the nutmeg and the tarragon on the mushrooms.

Reduce the heat to low and add the sour cream to the mushrooms. You may want to add a tablespoon or two of water to thin the sauce (or not). Mix in the sour cream thoroughly. Do not let it come to a simmer or boil or the sour cream will curdle. Stir in the beef and shallots. Add salt and pepper to taste.

Serve immediately over egg noodles, fettuccine, potatoes, or rice. (Potatoes, rice, and gluten-free pasta are gluten-free options.) Yield: Serves 4.

Beef with Onion Sauce

Ingredients

About 2 pounds of tenderized round or sirloin steak.

One package dry onion soup mix.

Salt and pepper or any seasoning you prefer.

Directions: Place your meat in a covered baking dish, sprinkle on the onion soup mix. Add a little water, about 1 cup to make sure the soup mix is all soaked. Bake for 1 1/2 to 2 hours on 325.This absolutely delicious, the meat is so tender it falls apart.

Number of Servings about 4

Chicken Breasts with Green Peppercorn Sauce
Ingredients
4 boneless skinless chicken breast halves
1 teaspoon safflower oil
¼ cup dry sherry
2 tablespoons minced onion
¼ cup white wine
½ cup 2% milk
1 tablespoon green peppercorns
¼ teaspoon dried tarragon
Directions: Preheat oven to 400 degrees F. In a large skillet over medium-high heat, sauté chicken breasts in safflower oil and sherry until lightly browned on both sides. Transfer to a baking dish. Bake for 15 minutes.
While chicken is baking, in the same skillet over medium heat, sauté onion in pan drippings until soft. Add wine, milk, peppercorns, and tarragon. Heat until sauce coats the back of a spoon. Serve over baked chicken. Makes 4 servings.

Southern Fried Catfish
Ingredients:
8 Catfish fillets (2 or 3 medium size pieces per person) any firm fish may be used.
1 cup White Corn Meal (or yellow)
1/3 cup all-purpose flour
2 teaspoons salt
1 teaspoon black pepper
1/2 teaspoon cayenne pepper
1/4 teaspoon garlic powder
2 medium eggs
1/4 cup buttermilk
Enough cooking oil to cover the fish (I use peanut or canola oil)

Directions:
Heat oil in a large, heavy frying pan over medium heat.
Combine all dry ingredients on a plate, mix well
Beat eggs and buttermilk together in a separate medium size bowl
Wash catfish fillets and pat dry.
Dip fillets in the egg wash, shake off excess then roll in the cornmeal mix to coat thoroughly on all sides.
Make sure oil is hot, (place handle of a wooden spoon in the oil. Bubbles should rise around the handle immediately. If not, the oil is not hot enough.)
Place the fish in the hot oil and fry until golden brown on both sides. Do not crowd the fish in the pan.
 Drain on paper towels and serve hot

Southern Cornbread Pie
For The Filling
Ingredients:
1 pound lean ground beef
1 large onion, coarsely chopped
1 can tomato soup
2 cups water
1 teaspoon salt (or to taste)
1 teaspoon black pepper (or to taste)
3 tablespoons chili powder
1/2 cup green pepper, chopped
1 can whole kernel corn, drained
Directions:
Brown beef and onion in skillet. Drain fat.
Add remaining ingredients, mix well. Simmer 15 minutes.
Transfer beef mixture to a 10 inch square baking dish and set aside.
For The Cornbread Topping
Ingredients:
3/4 cup cornmeal

1 tablespoon flour
1/2 tablespoon salt
1 1/2 tablespoons baking powder
1 egg
1/2 cup milk
1 tablespoon oil
Directions:
In a medium bowl, beat egg, oil and milk together until well blended.
Slowly add remaining dry ingredients and mix well.
Cooking Instructions
Pre heat oven to 350 degrees F.
Pour cornbread topping mix over top of beef mix in baking dish.
Bake in pre heated oven for 20-25 minutes or until top of cornbread
has browned. Serve steaming hot.

Chicken Cordon Bleu
Ingredients:
1/2 cup olive oil
1 1/4 pounds thin sliced boneless skinless chicken breast
5 ounces sliced ham
4 ounces sliced Swiss cheese
2 large eggs, beaten
2 cups Japanese (Panko) style bread crumbs
Lemon wedges (optional)
Directions
Heat 1/4 cup of the oil in large flat skillet over medium heat. Place
beaten eggs and bread crumbs in separate wide flat bowls and set
aside. Select and pair up the chicken breast cutlets equal in size; you'll
need 2 to make each schnitzel "sandwich" and depending on size, each
sandwich will serve 2 people generously - four for the whole recipe.
Place between wax paper using mallet pound to thin each to a
thickness of 1/4". Place a slice of ham on one of the thinned chicken
cutlets and on top of that a slice of Swiss cheese; trim the ham and

cheese to fit the chicken cutlet shape. Top with the matching thinned chicken cutlet to form the sandwich. At this point you may need to cut the sandwich in half to serving size, so it is easier to handle, coat and cook. Holding each sandwich firmly, dip it into beaten eggs coating one side completely; then carefully turn it over and dip the second side in eggs, allowing excess egg to drip away. In like manner coat both sides with bread crumbs. Place into heated oil in pan and fry til golden brown on both sides, adding the additional 1/4 cup oil as needed. Serve with lemon wedges (optional).

Chicken or Beef Pita
Ingredients
1 pita cut in half
2-3 slices of beef or chicken in each half of the pita
3 slices of cucumber in each pita
Add shredded lettuce to each pita
Put the dill sauce on inside each pita for a dressing Add garnish of lettuce, tomato, onion, and a pickle to the plate
Directions: To prepare the beef. Cut a beef steak into thin, long strips. Put those strips on the char broiler. Cook them medium well. To prepare the chicken, cut a cooked chicken breast into long strips cook the strips on the grill

Cajun Eggs
This is a great one skillet meal. When you are camping or fixing a breakfast for the boys, this is it. Hot, flavorful and filling
Ingredients
4 Eggs, cracked and whipped
6 oz of Andouille Sausage, ground or diced
½ Bell Pepper, cleaned and Julianne (Sliced)
¼ Red Onion, Cleaned and Sliced
¼ cup mix cheese / Cheddar and Jack
1 t. Butter

1T. Cajun Spice
Tabasco Sauce to Taste
8 Pita Bread Halves
Directions; In a 12 inch skillet on medium heat melt the butter add the sliced Bell peppers and onions. When peppers and onion are slightly cooked, should still be firm, add the Andouille Sausage, cook until nice and brown then add the eggs to the pan. With a fork keep moving the eggs so they don't burn in the pan. With eggs still a little runny add the cheese and Cajun spice, mix well until the eggs are cooked and firm.
Open the pita bread pockets add the Cajun eggs and top with Tabasco sauce to taste. Serve 8

Chicken and Sausage Jambalaya
Ingredients
6 to 8 ounces boneless, skinless chicken breast
1/2 pound smoked andouille or kielbasa sausage
1 pound of shrimp and / or crab meat
1 small onion, diced
1 stalk celery, diced
1 small clove garlic, minced
1 small bell pepper, diced
1 (28-ounce) can diced, peeled tomatoes
1 (28-ounce) Tomato sauce
1/2 teaspoon Tabasco sauce
2 cups of water
1/2 teaspoon gumbo filé powder
1 teaspoon Cajun spice
1 teaspoon Chicken and / or Beef base
2 cup of dry rice

Directions: Slice sausage into bite-sized pieces and brown in large pre-heated sauce pan (a cast-iron Dutch oven is ideal) over medium-high heat. Remove sausage from pan with slotted spoon and reserve drippings for next step. Wash chicken thoroughly and cut into 1/2-inch cubes. Sauté over medium-high heat (add a little peanut oil if there is not enough grease to sauté up to a total of about 2 tablespoons oil) until cooked through. Return sausage to pan and add onion, celery, red pepper and garlic. Sauté until vegetables are cooked through. Add Tabasco, add water, chicken and / or beef base and tomatoes and stir to combine. Add filé powder and Cajun spice. Simmer over low heat for about two hours. Add 2 cups of dry rice, simmer until rice is fully cooked. Add Tabasco to taste. You may serve the jambalaya in a shallow bowl with fresh cornbread or hushpuppies

Chuck Wagon Chili
Ingredients
6 pounds round steak, coarsely ground, diced / cubed
1 cup Olive Oil
1 3-oz bottle of Grandmas' Chili Powder
6 tablespoons cumin
6 small cloves garlic, minced
2 medium Red onions, chopped
6 dried chili pods, remove stems and seeds and boil 30 minutes in water
1-tablespoon oregano
2 tablespoons paprika
2 tablespoons Red wine vinegar
3 cups beef broth use beer instead of water
1 4-oz can diced Ortega green chilies
12 oz Stewed Tomatoes
Dash of Tabasco sauce or more to taste

Directions: Brown meat in Olive Oil, drain meat and add chili powder, cumin, garlic and chopped onions. Cook 30-45 minutes using as little liquid as possible; add water or beer only as necessary. Stir often. Remove skins from boiled pods, mash pulp and add to meat mixture, add oregano, paprika, vinegar, 2 cups of beef broth, Ortega green chiles, stewed tomatoes and Tabasco sauce. Simmer 30-45 minutes. Stir often. Serve with the best fresh bread you can find and enjoy... Note: Traditional Red Chili is defined by the International Chili Society as any kind of meat or combination of meats, cooked with red chili peppers, various spices and other ingredients, with the exception of BEANS and PASTA which are strictly forbidden.

Grilled Fillet Mignon
Ingredients
1 6 ounce fillet mignon
Directions: Marinate with very little extra virgin olive oil and seasoning salt. Place on hot grill. Cook both sides until done to your preference. **Note:** Regardless of the grade or cut, the fat in red meat is mostly saturated fat. This is the fat that your body turns into cholesterol. Always trim all visible fat from meat before cooking. Instead of gravy, base meats with broth, lemon juice or wine.
Cook meat and/or roast on a rack. The preferred methods are broiling, roasting, baking and grilling. Yield: 1 serving

Steak Maitre'D
Ingredients
3 teaspoons olive oil
8 ounces butterflied filet mignon
2 ounces brown sauce (Espanol or Bordelaise)
1/4 cup Worcestershire sauce
2 teaspoons Dijon mustard
3/4 cup freshly sliced mushrooms
3/4 cup freshly chopped tomatoes

1/3 cup freshly chopped scallions or green onions
1 tablespoon chopped shallots
Dash of Tabasco sauce
1 cup brandy
1/2 lemon
Directions: Over a gas flame, in a large, Teflon-coated skillet, heat the olive oil and add the filet. Then add the brown sauce, Worcestershire sauce, mustard, mushrooms, tomatoes, scallions, shallots and Tabasco sauce. Cook the filet for 3 minutes on each side. Add the brandy and lemon (squeeze lightly before adding). When brandy is hot, turn skillet over flame to ignite. Flambé and serve hot. Yield: 1 serving

Shrimp Diane
Ingredients
16 each, medium shrimp or prawns
1 cup stewed tomatoes
1/4 cup chopped green peppers
1 tablespoon olive oil
2 tablespoons Cajun spice
1 cup brandy
1/4 cup chopped onions
Directions: In a large skillet over open flame, add shrimp, Cajun spice and oil. Cook until shrimp is red and tender. Add peppers and onions and sauté until tender. Add brandy; heat and tip skillet until brandy ignites. Serve over rice. Yield: 6 - 8 servings

Grilled Shrimp / Serve with Mango Salsa
Ingredients
Large, raw, peeled, deveined shrimp (any number desired) your favorite spicy seasoning salt. I use "Spice It up Jalapeno Dusting Salt
Vegetable or olive oil to oil the pan
Sprinkle shrimp with seasoning salt and refrigerate until ready to grill.

Directions: Heat grill to medium, heating large cast iron skillet on grill. Brush skillet with oil just before cooking the shrimp. Add shrimp to skillet and cook until shrimp turn pink and opaque, urning each shrimp at least once, and allowing shrimp to brown slightly.

Mango Salsa
Ingredients
2 firm, ripe mangos, peeled and diced into ½ inch cubes
1 firm, ripe avocado, peeled and diced into ½ inch cubes added just before serving
½ cup diced red bell pepper
¼ cup diced red onion
¼ to 1 whole jalapeno pepper, seeded and diced fine
10 to 40 cilantro leaves (to taste)
3 Tbsp rice vinegar
1 Tbsp brown sugar
½ tsp salt
Directions: Mix all ingredients (except avocado) and refrigerate until ready to serve. Add avocado just prior to serving.

Salmon Baked in Foil
Ingreidents:
4 salmon fillets (about 5-6 ounces each)
4 cloves garlic, minced
6 Tbsp light olive oil
2 tsp dried basil (or 2 Tbsp fresh basil shredded)
2 tsp salt
2 tsp ground black pepper
2 Tbsp lemon juice
2 Tbsp fresh parsley, chopped
Directions
In a medium bowl, prepare the marinade by mixing the garlic, light olive oil, basil, salt, pepper, lemon juice and parsley. Place the salmon

fillets in a medium pyrex baking dish, and cover with the marinade. Marinate in the refrigerator for at least 1 hour, turning occasionally. Preheat oven to 375 F (190 degrees C).

Place the salmon fillets in large pieces of aluminum foil, cover with the marinade, and fold up the sides of the foil to completely seal. Place sealed salmon in the glass dish or on a baking sheet, and bake 35 minutes. Open one of the foils and check the salmon with a fork. If it flakes easily, it is done.

Server over rice or pasta, pouring the extra marinade from the foil over the fish

Shrimp Galveston
Ingredients
12 large jumbo shrimp, peeled and deveined (tail on or off)
1 onion cut into 1 inch pieces
1 bell pepper (red or green), cut into 1 inch pieces
2 lime wedges
4 Bamboo skewers
Marinade
Ingredients
1 cup corn oil
3 ounces lime juice
1 tablespoon fresh garlic, chopped fine
1 tablespoon Worcestershire sauce
1/4 cup chopped cilantro
Directions: Prepare marinade: Place all ingredients into a large bowl and mix together well. Divide shrimp, onions and bell peppers, and place on skewers. Place shrimp skewers in marinade making sure skewers are covered with marinade. Let sit for 20 minutes. Squeeze juice from lime wedges into a non-oiled pan. Place shrimp skewers in pan and fry until shrimp is white and tender. Serve over Spanish rice. Yield: 4 servings

Shrimp Scampi

This is a healthy alternative to the tradition shrimp scampi recipe

Ingredients

2 tablespoons crushed garlic

4 tablespoons extra virgin olive oil

2 pounds medium raw shrimp

1/8 cup lemon juice

2 cups orange juice

1/4 cup Marsala wine

1 tablespoon capers

4 tablespoons cornstarch

5 tablespoons cold water

2 teaspoons minced fresh basil

Lemon wedges

Directions: Shell and devein the shrimp leaving the tails on. In a large skillet, heat the olive oil and garlic. Add the orange juice, lemon juice, Marsala wine and heat until par-boiling. Add the cleaned shrimp. Cook over high heat shaking the pan and turning the shrimp once or twice until they turn pink (this should take about 5 minutes, depending on the size of the shrimp). Mix the cornstarch with water to make a paste. Add a little at a time and heat until the sauce is thick. Add the capers and stir well. Serve with lemon wedges and sprinkle with fresh basil. Yield: 6 - 8 servings

Shrimp Etouffee

Etouffe means, "Smothered" in gravy or a combination of seasoning, stock and vegetables. Chef Joe's Shrimp Etouffee follows this meaning by adding seafood stock and the "trilogy" of Cajun cooking onions, celery and green peppers. This is a lower fat recipe, which has the rich butter roux, left out, but retains the rich Cajun flavors.

Ingredients

¼ c. chopped red onions

¼ c. chopped celery

¼ c. green bell pepper
5 T. extra virgin olive oil
2 pounds cleaned uncooked whole
3 T. Cajun Seasoning
Medium shrimp
2 t. Chef Joe's Sicilian Seasoning
4 T. Seafood Stock*
Water as needed to thin
3 c. Tomato Puree
Louisiana style hot sauce to taste

Directions: Heat the olive oil in a large heavy skillet and add the onions, celery and bell peppers to the hot skillet. Cook until tender, and then add the shrimp. Cook until pink in color.

Then add the Seafood base, Cajun seasoning, and Chef Joe's Sicilian Seasoning.   With a wire whip add the tomato puree, reduce the heat, and simmer for 5 minutes. Add water if needed to thin sauce. Add hot sauce to taste or you may add more Cajun seasoning to taste. Remember real Cajun food does not burn your mouth: "If the last taste, tastes as good as the first, it's Cajun". Simmer Etouffee for about 10 minutes. Serve over rice immediately and enjoy!!! Serves 4 to 6.

* Seafood Stock - You can use any type of fish, clam, or lobster base. If you can't find the seafood base, use vegetable base

Scallops in Wine Sauce
Ingredients
2 cups bay scallops
1/4 cup butter
1 teaspoon Worcestershire sauce
1/4 cup minced onions
1/4 cup Marsala wine

Directions: Preheat oven to 500 degrees. Rinse and dry scallops. Divide scallops into large scallop shells or baking dishes. Melt butter in sauce pan. Add Worcestershire sauce. Add onion and cook until golden. Divide butter/onion mixture evenly over scallops. Add one tablespoon of wine to each. Bake for 10 minutes. Serve at once. Yield: 4 servings

Low Calorie Halibut Steak
Ingredients
2 tablespoons olive oil
1 tea spoon fresh garlic, chopped
1/4 cup orange juice
1/4 cup Marsala wine (optional)
1 teaspoon lemon juice
Pinch of white pepper
1 tablespoon capers
4   6 ounce halibut steaks
Directions: Heat oil and garlic in a skillet. Add orange juice, wine, lemon juice, white pepper and capers. Bring to a simmer. Add halibut steaks and cook on each side 2-3 minutes until white and tender. Serve with white rice. Yield: 4 servings

Roast Turkey
Ingredients
1   12 pound turkey
4 tablespoons seasoning salt
1 tablespoon garlic powder
1 quart water
1 stick butter
Directions: Remove turkey neck and giblets and use to make gravy. Rinse turkey under running cold water. Pat dry inside and out. Season cavities with butter -- rub generously. Loosely fill neck and body cavities with apple cornbread stuffing. Do not pack stuffing as it will

expand during cooking. Brush bird all over with melted butter. Season with seasoned salt and garlic powder. Place breast side up on rack in roasting pan. Add water and cover. Place in a preheated 350 degree oven for 3 hours. Uncover and cook 30 minutes or until golden brown (internal temperature must be 185 degrees or higher). Let turkey stand 10 - 15 minutes before carving.

Steak Luzon
Originally developed by a Pilipino chef at Sherman's Restaurant, Alhambra, California. It's maybe Asian or Pilipino, but it's American to me.
Ingredients
2 pounds round steak
1 cup Worcestershire sauce
1 cup soy sauce
1 bunch diced green onions
2 medium diced green bell peppers
3 medium diced tomatoes
2 tablespoons crushed garlic
Directions: Cut round steak into 1/4 by 1/4 inch cubes (bite size). In medium size sauce pan, place Worcestershire sauce, soy sauce and green onions. Add meat, cover and simmer until meat is tender. Add more sauce, if needed.
When meat is tender, add diced bell peppers. Cook for 15 minutes or until peppers are tender. Reduce heat and add tomatoes. Cover for 5 minutes and serve. Serve over rice pilaf or white rice. Yield: 8 servings

Roasted Quail
Ingredients
3 cups Marsala wine
1/2 cup sugar
1-1/2 tablespoons whole black pepper corns
6 medium pears, peeled, stems left on; cut bottoms to form straight

cut
20 each quail
1-1/2 cups butter
2/3 cup red onions
1-1/2 cups beef broth
Directions: In a 4 - 5 quart pan, combine wine, sugar, peppers, and pears. Bring to boil, cover and simmer, turning pears several times until tender when pierced. Set aside in a warm place.
Rinse birds inside and out and pat dry. Melt 4 - 6 tablespoons of butter in a 10 - 12 inch frying pan over medium high heat. Add birds without crowding; turn to brown all sides. Arrange birds, breast up and slightly apart on racks in two roasting pans. Roast birds in a 400 degree oven until breast meat near bone is still moist (internal temperature 160 degrees). Drain juices from birds in pan. Pour pan drippings into frying pan. Add onions and stir over heat for two minutes. Add broth and 1-1/2 cups of the pear poaching liquid. Boil rapidly until sauce is reduced to 1-1/3 cups. Turn heat to low and add remaining butter all at once. Stir constantly until butter melts and blends into sauce. Pour sauce through a strainer into a small bowl. Ladle sauce over birds.

Yankee Pot Roast
Ingredients
5 pounds beef chuck roast
1 diced red onion
1 teaspoon minced garlic
1 teaspoon chopped dried parsley
1 bay leaf
1 teaspoon dried thyme
1 quart apple juice
8 ounces tomato paste
1 teaspoon salt
1 teaspoon black pepper
16 ounces water

Directions: Brown meat in a stock pot. When the meat is browned, add the remaining ingredients. (Sufficient water to cover may be added.) Simmer slowly for 4 hours. Remove meat and strain the juice. Reduce the juice to a proper consistency for gravy. Yield: 10 servings

Spambalaya
Ingredients
1 (12 ounce) can SPAM Luncheon Meat, cubed
1 cup chopped onion
2/3 cup chopped celery
2 cloves garlic, minced
1 (14-1/2 ounce) can Cajun style or regular stewed tomatoes
1 (10-3/4 ounce) can lower sodium chicken broth
1/2 teaspoon dried leaf thyme
6 to 8 drops hot pepper sauce
1 cup rice
2 tablespoons chopped parsley
Directions: In lagre non-stick skillet or 3-quart non-stick saucepan, saute SPAM
Luncheon Meat, onion, green pepper, celery, and garlic until vegetables
are tender. Add tomatoes, chicken broth, thyme, hot pepper sauce, and
bay leaves. Bring to a boil; stir in the rice. Cover.
Reduce heat and simmer 20 minutes or until rice is tender. Discard bay leaves. Sprinkle with parsley. Makes 6 servings.

Spam Wellington
Ingredients
1 can biscuit dough
1/2 cup brown sugar
Directions: Preheat oven to 350. Place SPAM, as close together as possible on cookie sheet. Sprinkle with brown sugar. Pop biscuit dough can. Cover SPAM with dough. Mash edges of dough together with fingertips so that SPAM is not exposed. Bake for 30 minutes or until dough is golden brown. Let stand 10 minutes before carving

Meatless Jambalaya
Ingredients
1 lb. Meatless Chorizo
3 T. Extra virgin olive oil
2 t. vegetable stock
1 ½ cups of chopped celery
1 ½ cups of chopped bell pepper
1 ½ cup of chopped red onion
1 ½ t. minced garlic
4 cups of peeled and chopped tomatoes
¾ cup tomato sauce
½ cup chopped green onions
2 cups cooked converted rice
2 T. Cajun spice & Louisiana hot sauce to taste
Directions: In a large skillet sauté' the Chorizo until crisp. Add the celery, peppers, onions and garlic sauté' until tender yet firm. Add the vegetable stock and chopped tomatoes and tomato sauce and Cajun seasoning, simmer for 20 minutes. Add Louisiana style hot sauce to tastes serve over rice and top with green onions.

Vegetarian Irish Stew
Ingredients
2 medium onions
¼ cup unbleached flour
4 cups water
1 cup carrots or 1 cup parsnips, sliced
1 cup turnips or 1 cup rutabagas
1 cup celery, diced
½ cup split red lentils
½ cup fresh parsley
¼ cup soy sauce
3 vegetable bouillon cubes
1 bay leaves
2 teaspoons marmite
1 teaspoon sugar
¼ teaspoon thyme
¼ teaspoon rosemary
¼ teaspoon marjoram
pepper
1 cup textured vegetable protein, chunks
Directions: In a large, lightly oiled pot steam fry the onion until it begins to soften [that means cook it in a bit of water] Add flour and stir around completely. Add the remaining ingredients, mix well, bring to boil. Cover and simmer on low for 30 minutes or until vegetables are done. Taste and season. Note: The turnips should be large dice. The carrots round sliced. You may use other yeast extract than marmite.

Vegetarian Shepherd's Pie
Ingredients
1 1/2 cups low-sodium vegetable broth
1/3 cup dry red wine
1 tablespoon **tomato paste**
1 tablespoon **all-purpose flour**

3 pounds **russet potatoes**, peeled, and cut into large dice
5 tablespoons **unsalted butter**
2 pounds fresh sliced zucchini
Salt and freshly ground black pepper
1/2 medium yellow onion, finely chopped
3 medium celery stalks, finely chopped
5 medium **garlic cloves**, finely chopped
1 medium **celery root**, peeled and small dice
3 medium **carrots**, peeled and small dice
2 medium **parsnips**, peeled and small dice
1 tablespoon finely chopped fresh sage leaves
1 tablespoon finely chopped fresh thyme leaves
2/3 cup whole milk

Directions

In a medium bowl, whisk together broth, wine, tomato paste, and flour until evenly combined and smooth.

Place potatoes in a large pot and cover with heavily salted water by 2 inches. Bring potatoes to a boil and cook until fork tender, about 20 to 30 minutes.

Heat the oven on broil and place a rack in the upper third. Meanwhile, melt 1 tablespoon of the butter in a 3 to 4-quart Dutch oven (or oven-ready saucepan) over medium-high heat. When it foams, add half the zucchini and cook, stirring rarely, until zucchini are browned, about 5 minutes. Remove zucchini from pan, season well with salt and freshly ground black pepper, and set aside. Repeat to cook off remaining zucchini.

Return pan to stove over medium heat and add 1 tablespoon of the butter, onion, celery, and garlic, and cook until softened and golden, about 2 minutes. Add celery root, carrot, parsnip, and herbs, and season well with salt and freshly ground black pepper. Cook until browned and softened, about 6 minutes.

Add wine mixture to pan and deglaze by stirring and scraping up any browned bits. Let cook until simmering and slightly thickened, about 3 minutes. Stir in reserved zucchini and any juices that have accumulated and simmer until slightly thickened, about 8 minutes. Remove from heat and reserve in pan.

When potatoes are ready, drain well. Return to pan and mash until uniformly smooth. Fold in remaining 2 tablespoons butter and milk, and season well with salt and freshly ground black pepper. If necessary, keep warm over low heat.

Dot potatoes over vegetable mixture and spread to edges of pan to cover completely. Rough up the surface of the potatoes so there are bits that will get browned and crunchy. Bake until top is golden, about 15 to 20 minutes. Serve

Smokin' BBQ Pork Chili Rub
This rub is heavy on the chili powder and cumin and contains liquid smoke to enhance the smokiness of your barbecue.

Ingredients
1 cup cumin seeds crushed
1/3 cup minced garlic
3 tablespoon coarse salt
1 tablespoon cayenne pepper
1 tablespoon seasoning salt
3 tablespoon of chili powder
1/4 cup liquid smoke to be rubbed on the ribs prior to adding the dry rub
3 pounds of pork spareribs

Directions: Prepare ribs by removing the membrane from the underside of the ribs. Trim off any loose fat or meat. Prepare smoker or grill. You will want to hold a temperature around 200 degrees F. for 4 to 6 hours so plan accordingly. Season with Smokin' Chili Rub and place on grill or in smoker. While ribs are cooking, prepare barbecue sauce. Cook ribs until the internal temperature of the meat reaches about 145 degrees F. The last 15 minutes of cooking brush with barbecue sauce continually then serve hot and juicy.

Bagna Calda
Ingredients
large jug of olive oil (51 oz is what I used)
1 pound of butter
1 can anchovies
5 heads of garlic
large shrimp
chicken breast
steak
Cauliflower
Broccoli
Carrots
Brussels' Sprouts
Baby Red Potatoes
Baby Corn
Artichoke Hearts (packed in water)
Crusty French Bread (the best bet is to get it at a local bakery rather than the grocery)
Directions: In a large electric skillet, combine olive oil and butter, turn heat on low (200-250) let that melt together while you prepare the anchovies and garlic. Cut up the anchovies into little pieces. Peel and chop garlic. (Chopped is better than pressed or crushed in this recipe.) Mix it all together and simmer until garlic and anchovies are fully cooked. (I like to simmer for a few hours... on VERY LOW so it doesn't burn). When the guests arrive (or when you are ready to eat). Have the meat and veggies out and ready to go. Start out with a few pieces of each food cook until done, and replace as you take it out. Serve on crusty French bread and eat like a sandwich.

Braised Short Ribs

Ingredients

3 to 4 pounds short ribs cut in 3-inch pieces

Salt and pepper

1/2 cup flour

2 tablespoons Extra Virgin Olive Oil

2 cups apple cider

1 1/2 cups crushed tomatoes

1 teaspoon dried leaf rosemary

1/2 teaspoon dried thyme

1 large onion, coarsely chopped

1 clove garlic, minced

1 medium onion, chopped

1 cup baby carrots

1 cup sliced celery

10 leaves chopped fresh basil

1 cup of tomato paste

Directions: Heat oven to 300°. Sprinkle ribs with salt and pepper; toss with the flour. In a roasting pan*, heat oil (over 2 burners, if possible) over medium heat. Add the short ribs in 1 layer. Cook, turning frequently, until well browned. If necessary, the ribs can be browned in a Dutch oven, turning frequently. Continue with adding cider and crushed tomato's, the large coarsely chopped onion, and herbs, then transfer to a roasting pan if the Dutch oven isn't ovenproof. Cover and bake for 3 1/2 hours. Remove short ribs from the pan and strain the broth into a large saucepan or Dutch oven. Skim off excess fat; bring to a boil, uncovered, then reduce heat to medium, add the tomato paste to thicken and simmer for 5 minutes, uncovered. Add the remaining onion, celery, and carrots to the sauce. Cover and cook over medium heat until vegetables are tender. Return the short ribs to the sauce and heat through. Garnish with Fresh Basil to serve

Braciole
Serves: 4 servings

Ingredients
1/2 cup dried Italian-style bread crumbs
1 garlic clove, minced
2/3 cup grated **Romano**
1/3 cup grated **provolone**
2 tablespoons chopped fresh Italian parsley leaves
4 tablespoons olive oil
Salt and freshly ground black pepper
1 (1 1/2-pound) **flank steak**
1 cup dry white **wine**
3 1/4 cups Simple Tomato Sauce, recipe follows, or store-bought
marinara sauce

Directions
Stir the first 5 ingredients in a medium bowl to **blend**. Stir in 2 tablespoons of the oil. Season mixture with salt and pepper and set aside.
Lay the flank steak flat on the work surface. Sprinkle the bread crumb mixture evenly over the steak to cover the top evenly. Starting at 1 short end, roll up the steak as for a jelly roll to enclose the filling completely. Using butcher's twine, tie the steak roll to secure. Sprinkle the braciole with salt and pepper.
Preheat the oven to 350 degrees
Heat the remaining 2 tablespoons of oil in a heavy large ovenproof skillet over medium heat. Add the braciole and cook until browned on all sides, about 8 minutes. Add the wine to the pan and bring to a boil. Stir in the marinara sauce. Cover partially with foil and bake until the meat is almost tender, turning the braciole and basting with the sauce every 30 minutes. After 1 hour, uncover and continue baking until the meat is tender, about 30 minutes longer. The total cooking time should be about 1 1/2 hours.

Remove the braciole from the sauce. Using a large sharp knife, cut the braciole crosswise and diagonally into 1/2-inch-thick slices. Transfer the slices to plates. Spoon the sauce over and serve.

Simple Tomato Sauce:
1/2 cup extra-virgin olive oil
1 small onion, chopped
2 cloves garlic, chopped
1 stalk celery, chopped
1 carrot, chopped
2 (32-ounce) cans crushed **tomatoes**
4 to 6 basil leaves
2 dried bay leaves
Sea salt and freshly ground black pepper
4 tablespoons unsalted butter, optional
Directions:
In a large casserole pot, heat oil over medium-high heat. Add onion and garlic and sauté until soft and translucent, about 2 minutes. Add celery and carrot and season with salt and pepper. Sauté until all the vegetables are soft, about 5 minutes. Add tomatoes, **basil**, and bay leaves and reduce the heat to low. Cover the pot and **simmer** for 1 hour or until thick. Remove bay leaves and taste for seasoning. If sauce tastes too acidic, add unsalted butter, 1 tablespoon at a time, to round out the flavor.
Pour half the tomato sauce into the bowl of a **food processor**. Process until smooth. Continue with remaining tomato sauce. If not using all the sauce, allow it to cool completely and then pour 1 to 2 cup portions into plastic freezer bags. Freeze for up to 6 months.

Black Pepper Fettuccine
Ingredients
1 pound fettuccini cooked al dente
1 pint whipping cream
1/2 cup roux
2 teaspoons tomato paste
2 teaspoons black pepper
3 large cooked prawns
1 cup Marsala wine
3 tablespoons Cajun seasoning
1 cup Parmesan cheese
1 cup smoked sausage
Directions: In a large skillet add whipping cream. Heat until boiling.
Add Marsala wine, Cajun seasoning, parmesan cheese, tomato paste
and black pepper. Heat until par-boiling. Add roux and cook until thick.
Add sausage and fettuccini. Heat and add cooked prawns to garnish.
Roux: Heat butter or oil in a large heavy skillet over high heat until it
begins to smoke. Add 1/2 cup of flour whisking constantly until a thick
paste forms. Roux should be light red brown to black. Yield: 4 servings

Chicken Cacciatore
Ingredients
4 each whole boneless skinless chicken breasts
1 cup Joe's Spaghetti Sauce
1 each sliced green bell pepper
1 each sliced red bell pepper
1 each sliced yellow onion
4 large sliced mushrooms
1 cup grated mozzarella cheese
1 cup grated cheddar cheese
2 tablespoons crushed garlic
3 tablespoons olive oil

Directions: Sauté the garlic, bell peppers, onions and mushrooms in olive oil until tender. Cover each piece of chicken breast with 1/4 of the sautéed mixture. Cover with spaghetti sauce and cheese. Bake in 350 degree oven on a cookie sheet for 20 minutes or until chicken is white and tender.

Chicken Marsala
Ingredients
6 chicken breast
1 cup of flour
2 t. oregano
2 t. Basil
2 t. garlic powder
2 t. Italian Parsley
2 T. Extra Virgin olive oil
 c Marsala Wine
1 t. crushed garlic
1 t. margarine
¼ cup sliced mushrooms
Directions: Cut the boneless breast in half lengthwise, and place between sheets of plastic wrap. Gently flatten with a mallet, and trim off any rough edges. Mix all the spices into the flour and dredge the chicken lightly into the flour until completely covered. Heat the olive oil and crushed garlic in a skillet add the chicken and let cook until light brown then turn over, add the margarine and simmer on low heat. When chicken is firm to the touch add the Marsala wine and mushrooms. Simmer until mushrooms are tender. Serve over Polenta, Risotto or Pasta with fresh vegetables. Serves 6

Chicken Parmesan
Ingredients
6 chicken breast
1 cup of Bread crumbs
2 t. oregano
2 t. Dried Basil
2 t. garlic powder
2 t. Italian Parsley
2 t. Parmesan Cheese
4 T. Extra Virgin olive oil
1 cup red marinara sauce
1 cup shredded Mozzarella cheese
Dash of Parmesan for garnish
Directions: Cut the boneless breast in half lengthwise, and place between sheets of plastic wrap. Gently flatten with a mallet, and trim off any rough edges. Mix all the spices and 2 t. Parmesan cheese into the breadcrumbs and dredge the chicken lightly into the breadcrumbs until completely covered. Heat the olive oil in a skillet add the chicken and let cook until light brown then turn over. When chicken is firm to the touch and lightly brown color remove from pan. Heat the marinara sauce cover the chicken lightly with one large spoon full, top lightly with mozzarella sauce and a dash of Parmesan cheese. Serve hot. Serve over Polenta, Risotto or Pasta with fresh vegetables.

Chicken Breasts Parmesan
 Ingredients:
1 8 ounce can tomato sauce
1 tea spoon Italian seasoning
1/4 teaspoon garlic salt
1/4 teaspoon pepper
1/3 cup bread or corn flake crumbs
1/4 cup grated Parmesan cheese
1 teaspoon dried parsley flakes

1 egg, beaten
2 large boneless chicken breasts (if small, use 4)
1/2 cup shredded mozzarella cheese (2 ounces)
Directions: Mix tomato sauce, Italian seasoning, garlic salt and pepper in a microwave safe container. Cover with waxed paper. Microwave at high (100%) for 2 minutes. Stir. Reduce to power to medium (50%) and microwave 5 minutes more, stirring once. Remove and set aside. Mix crumbs, Parmesan cheese and parsley flakes. Dip chicken in egg, then in crumb mixture. Place in a baking dish (10 inch square or 12" x 8"). Cover with waxed paper. Microwave at medium high (70%) until chicken is tender, approximately 9-14 minutes. Rearrange chicken half way through the cooking cycle (do not turn over!). Pour sauce over chicken. Sprinkle mozzarella cheese over chicken and then sprinkle with Parmesan cheese. Microwave at medium high (70%) until mozzarella cheese melts and sauce is hot, approximately 2 to 5-1/2 minutes).Yield: 2 servings

Chicken Piccata
Ingredients
2 skinless and boneless chicken breasts, butterflied and then cut in half
Sea salt and freshly ground black pepper
All-purpose flour, for dredging
6 tablespoons unsalted butter
5 tablespoons extra-virgin olive oil
1/3 cup fresh lemon juice
1/2 cup chicken stock
1/4 cup brined capers, rinsed
1/3 cup fresh parsley, chopped
Directions
Season chicken with salt and pepper. Dredge chicken in flour and shake off excess.

In a large skillet over medium high heat, melt 2 tablespoons of butter with 3 tablespoons olive oil. When butter and oil start to sizzle, add 2 pieces of chicken and cook for 3 minutes. When chicken is browned, flip and cook other side for 3 minutes. Remove and transfer to plate. Melt 2 more tablespoons butter and add another 2 tablespoons olive oil. When butter and oil start to sizzle, add the other 2 pieces of chicken and brown both sides in same manner. Remove pan from heat and add chicken to the plate.

Into the pan add the lemon juice, stock and capers. Return to stove and bring to boil, scraping up brown bits from the pan for extra flavor. Check for seasoning. Return all the chicken to the pan and simmer for 5 minutes. Remove chicken to platter. Add remaining 2 tablespoons butter to sauce and whisk vigorously. Pour sauce over chicken and garnish with parsley.

Chilean Sea Bass with sea Beans and Basil Tomato Broth
Ingredients:
7 oz Chilean Sea Bass Fillet very fresh skin off;
3 oz sea beans
1 oz Alpha Alpha Sprouts as garnish
2 Spring of Thyme
1 Scallion Finely Chopped
1 Tsp Fresh Italian parsley leaves Finely chopped
1 tsp extra virgin Olive Oil
Salt and pepper to season
1 Nasturtium Flower for the finish
For the broth :
1 Quart of water
2 Ripe Tomato on the vine diced
6 Leaves Fresh Basil
1/2 Spanish onion diced
2 Tbs Chopped Celery Root
1 garlic clove whole

1 Tsp Salt

1/2 Tsp fresh Ground Black Pepper

Directions

Prapare the broth :

Pour the quart of cold water in a medium pot add all the ingredients, bring to boil and then dim the fire and let gently simmer for one hour (if reduces too much add a little more of hot water);

After the hour use an immersion blender and grind all the ingredients in the pot than let simmer for 30 min more, don't let it reduce too much, than strain the broth with a fine strainer season as needed and keep it hot; Set on a working table one Sheet of Parchment Paper big enough to wrap the fish filet ; Put the fish filet in the middle of the parchment paper sprinkle with salt and pepper ; Top the fish fillet with the thyme, the scallion and the parsley; Drizzle with the extra virgin olive oil; Wrap the fish in the parchment paper (as you were wrapping a gift) Fold one side of the paper on the other than fold the sides . Save the wrap as made in the fridge for 15 min.

In a small pot of boiling water and NO SALT blanch the sea beans for 4 minutes than shock them in iced water so they won't loose the color .(test them if they are too salty blanch them again for two more minute in fresh boiling water)Set aside; Cook the fish in a preheated oven at 350 F for 13/15 min mean while reheat the sea beans in boiling water for one minute;

The Plate :

Pour the Broth in an Individual peacher and keep it hot;

Unwrap the fish carefully and clean it from all the garnish used in the cooking wrap;

Place the hot sea beans in a nice big pasta bowl , top with the fish and garnish with the sprouts and the Nasturtium flower than gently pour the broth all around the fish finish with a little drizzle of Extra virgin olive oil just on the fish.

Papa Joe's Spaghetti Sauce
The sauce is rich in flavor and thickness. It retains lots of flavor from the pork roast. Be sure to cook you pasta al a dente, never over cook the pasta, it needs to be firm and fresh.
Ingredients:
2- 1 pound cans tomato puree
2- Small cans tomato paste cups water
1 - Cup dry Marsala wine
1   tablespoon sweet basil
2   tablespoon chopped oregano
2   tablespoon fresh chopped garlic
2   tablespoon chopped parsley
2   bay leaves
1   cup of diced red onion
1/3 cup olive oil
1/2 cup sugar
2 pounds pork roast
Salt to taste
Directions: In a large saucepan, add the olive oil and diced onions, sauté for just a few minutes, and then add the chopped garlic. Sauté 2 minutes add the pork roast and lightly brown on each side. Empty tomato puree and paste into a saucepan. Add all spices, sugar, water and wine. Mix very well cook for 4 - 5 hours until internal temperature of pork is 160 to 180 degrees. Serve hot over your favorite pasta. The main ingredient is the pork. It flavors the sauce as it cooks. You can use pig's feet, pork or pork tenderloin or just boneless pork ribs.

Sicilian Chicken Pasta
Ingredients
1 Pound small Penne
3 boneless, skinless Chicken Breast, sliced thin
1/2 Jar: Artichoke Hearts in Oil drained and chopped
2 Tablespoons Each: Small Capers
½ cup Tomato Puree
2-4 Cloves Garlic, smashed and minced
1/3 cup Extra Virgin Olive Oil
Large Pinch Each: Dried Rosemary, Dried Basil, Dried Oregano, Ground Hot Peppers, Sea Salt, Fresh Ground Pepper
Fresh Basil for garnish
Directions: Cook penne until al dente. Rinse with cold water, set aside Heat oil in the wok on medium heat. When olive oil is hot but not smoking, add garlic. When garlic is fragrant, add the chicken. When chicken is fully cooked and firm, add the tomato puree, rosemary, basil, oregano, chile flakes, artichoke hearts, seasoned peppers and capers. Sauté, stirring frequently. Add salt and pepper to taste. Add the cooked and drained pasta to the skillet. Serve with grated cheese if desired.

Roasted Chicken with
Prosciutto and Kalamata Olives
Ingredients
1 chicken, 3 1/2-4 lbs.
1/4 lb. prosciutto, in one piece, diced into 1/2-inch cubes
1/3 cup shallots, minced
2 cloves garlic, minced
1/2 cup whole Kalamata Olives, unpitted, diced Keep a few whole for garnish
1/2 cup Marsala wine
All seasoning salt (I prefer Lawry's) to taste
6 fresh basil leaves, chopped

Directions: Preheat the oven to 350°F. With a sharp heavy knife, split the chicken down the backbone and open it up. Turn it breast side up and flatten with the palm of your hand. Cut a slit in the skin at the bottom of the breast and slip the "ankles" of the chicken through the slit. Sprinkle liberally with all purpose seasoning salt. Transfer the chicken, breast side down, to a lightly oiled roasting pan, best to use olive oil spray. Bake for 45 minutes. While the chicken is baking, prepare and combine the prosciutto, shallots, garlic and olives.

Remove the chicken from the oven and transfer to a plate. Remove any accumulated fat from the roasting pan. Scatter the prosciutto mixture evenly in the roasting pan and add the Marsala wine. Place the chicken skin side up into the pan. Bake for 45 minutes longer. Remove the chicken from the pan. Either carve the chicken or cut it up into serving pieces. Pour the prosciutto mixture over the chicken and serve. Garnish with the whole Kalamata olives and sprinkle with chopped fresh basil for garnish. Serves 3-4

Popeyed Pesto Chicken
This is simple heart healthy chicken dish that can be served with rice, or just by itself. It has lots of flavor and lots of nutriments.
Ingredients
4 boneless skinless chicken breast
3 t. Extra virgin olive oil
½ t. crushed garlic
Fresh Spinach
1 cup Chardonnay wine
Seasoning salt to taste
Directions: Sautee' spinach in 1 teaspoon of olive oil until very slightly wilted. Place the raw chicken breast in a freezer baggie, seal. On a chopping board using a meat mallet pound the chicken on both sides until thin. Remove from bag, lay out and spread pesto sauce on the

chicken then take a little cooked spinach lay over pesto sauce on to chicken. Sprinkle with seasoning salt and roll. With a tooth pick secure chicken. Add the remainder of olive oil into medium size skilled, heat adds crushed garlic and chicken, cook for a few minutes turning chicken until brown on all sides. Add the wine. Cover and let cook 10 minutes or until the chicken if full cooked and tender. Slice chicken and fan out on plate, garnish with fresh basil leaf. Serve with Pasta, rice or couscous.

Ciabatta Deli Sandwiches with
Pepperoncini and Artichokes
Make these sandwiches when you don't want to turn on the stove.
Ingredients
1 6-ounce jar marinated artichoke hearts, drained, coarsely chopped
1/4 cup (packed) sliced peperoncini plus 5 teaspoons juice from jar
3 tablespoons chopped white onion
2 tablespoons drained capers
2 tablespoons chopped fresh oregano
2 teaspoons chili-garlic sauce
2 ciabatta rolls, halved horizontally
4 ounces sliced provolone cheese
6 ounces assorted sliced deli meats (such as soppressata, prosciutto, and salami)
1 1/2 cups (packed) fresh arugula
Directions: Mix artichoke hearts, peperoncini with juice from jar, onion, capers, oregano, and chili-garlic sauce in small bowl; season to taste with pepper. Arrange rolls, cut side up, on work surface; spread artichoke mixture over, dividing equally. Divide provolone cheese, then deli meats and arugula, between the bottom 2 halves. Cover with roll tops. Cut each sandwich diagonally in half and serve.

Eggplant Bayou
Ingredients
3 medium eggplant
1/4 cup chopped celery
3/4 cup Italian bread crumbs
1/8 teaspoon minced garlic
1/2 pound medium shrimp
3/4 cup milk
1/4 cup chopped onions
1/4 cup chopped green peppers
2 medium eggs
1/2 pound crab meat
1/4 cup diced green onions
2 tablespoons Cajun seasoning
Directions
Cut eggplant in half. Heat skillet with oil. In mixing bowl whip eggs and milk. Whittle out the pulp of the eggplant halves and cut small piece of eggplant on the bottom so it will sit straight. Dip eggplant into eggs, then dip into bread crumbs. Place into hot skillet and brown all sides.In a small skillet, sauté celery, onions, peppers and garlic until tender. Add crab meat and Cajun seasoning. Add to eggplant. Sauté peeled shrimp until red and tender. Top eggplant and bake for 10 minutes. Serve hot. Yield: 6 servings

Fettuccine Alfredo
Ingredients
½ cup margarine
½ cup of flour
2 pints of ½ & ½ milk
1 pound fresh fettuccine
1 cup freshly grated parmesan cheese
1/4 cup Marsoaa wine
3 teaspoon chicken base

½ Teaspoon fresh minced garlic

1/2 teaspoon chopped fresh basil

Directions: Cook the fettuccine and rinse with cold water and drain, set aside.

In a large, heavy saucepan, melt the margarine over low heat and add the flour. Mix margarine and flour together until a paste (Roux) is formed, and then slowly add the ½ & ½. Heat until sauce is thick. With sauce on very low heat and stir in the cheese, wine, chicken base and garlic until thick and tasty, add more wine if sauce is to thick. Pour pasta into pan, mix quickly and serve immediately. Sprinkle basil on top. Yield: 4 - 6 servings

Fettuccine Jambalaya

Ingredients

2 tablespoons Cajun spice

3 tablespoons butter

½ pound andouille sausage

¼ pound cooked peeled shrimp

½ cup chopped red onions

½ cup chopped celery

½ cup chopped green bell peppers

½ tablespoons minced garlic

¼ cup canned tomato puree

½ cup chopped tomatoes

1 cup chicken stock

Tabasco to taste

Directions: Melt the butter in a saucepan over high heat. Add the sausage, cook until meat turns brown. Add the peppers, celery, onions and garlic, cooked until tender. Add the chicken stock, tomato puree and chopped tomatoes. Add the shrimp, reduce heat and simmer for 15 minutes. Serve hot add Tabasco to taste. Yield: 4 serving

Italian Style Meat Balls
Ingredients
2 pounds lean ground beef
1 cup Italian style seasoned bread crumbs
2 eggs, beaten
1 tablespoon garlic powder
1/2 teaspoon chopped dried parsley
1 teaspoon ground oregano
Directions: Preheat oven to 350 F. In a large bowl, mix all the ingredients together. Roll mixture into balls approximately 1 inch in diameter. Bake in oven until done ~ meat balls should be brown on all sides and firm to the touch when ready. Serve hot. Yield: 12 meatballs.

Nana's Eggplant Lasagna

Ingredients
2 large **eggplants**, sliced lengthwise 3/4-inch thick (8 slices)
5 tablespoons olive oil, divided plus more for baking dish
Coarse salt and freshly ground black pepper
2 **garlic cloves**, minced
1 tablespoon freshly chopped basil leaves
1 (15-ounce) container **whole milk ricotta cheese**
1 lb of shredded mozzarella.
1 cup grated Parmesan, divided
2 tablespoons freshly chopped **oregano** leaves
2 cups Nona's Marinara Sauce, recipe follows

Directions
Preheat oven to 400 degrees F.
Arrange sliced eggplant in a single layer on 2 sheet pans. Brush on both sides using 3 tablespoons of olive oil and season with salt and pepper. Roast the eggplant until it is soft and golden. Turn slices halfway through, about 25 minutes.

In a large bowl add the ricotta, mozzarella, 1/2 cup Parmesan, basil, oregano, garlic 2 teaspoons of salt and 1/4 teaspoon pepper. Mix well. Brush an 8-inch baking dish with oil.
Spread half of the marinara sauce on the bottom of the prepared baking dish. Lay 4 slices on top followed by the ricotta mixture. Lay another 4 slices of eggplant and finish with marinara sauce. Top with the remaining 1/2 cup Parmesan. Bake until golden brown, at 350 degrees, for 30 minutes.

Italian Chicken Skillet
Ingredients:
1 lb. boneless skinless chicken breast
1 green pepper
1 small red onion
1 can diced Roma tomatoes
1 cup water
1 pkg. Macaroni & Cheese Dinner
Directions:
Cook and stir chicken in large skillet sprayed with cooking spray on medium-high heat 5 min. or until chicken is no longer pink. Add peppers and onions; cook and stir 5 min. or until chicken is done. Stir in tomatoes, water and Macaroni. Bring to boil; cover. Simmer on low heat 10 min. or until macaroni is tender, stirring occasionally. Add Cheese Sauce; stir until blended.

Pasta Primavera
Ingredients
1 pound cooked pasta (your choice)
4 tablespoons extra virgin olive oil
2 tablespoons minced garlic
1/2 cup Parmesan cheese
1 each diced red bell pepper
1 each sliced zucchini
2 each diced roma tomatoes
1/2 cup diced black olives
2 tablespoons pine nuts
1 teaspoon freshly chopped basil
Directions: Cook pasta until tender; drain and mix lightly with two tablespoons of olive oil and set aside. In skillet, sauté the zucchini and bell pepper in three tablespoons of olive oil and garlic. Cook until tender. Add the black olives, then the pasta and stir fry until hot. Add the roma tomatoes, fold in gently. Serve hot and garnish with pine nuts and fresh basil. Sprinkle with Parmesan cheese. Yield: 4 servings

Linguine of the Sea
Ingredients
1 pound fresh bay scallops
2 tablespoons lemon juice
1 tablespoon clam juice
1 tablespoon minced fresh garlic
1/2 cup Marsala wine
Pinch of white pepper
1 cup heavy cream
8-10 sliced, canned artichoke hearts
1 cup grated parmesan cheese
1/2 cup clams
1 pound cooked linguine

Directions: Cook linguine as you would any pasta, drain and place into cool water. Wash scallops thoroughly under cold water and drain well. Set skillet over medium heat, wait 1 minute and add Marsala wine, lemon juice, clam juice, fresh garlic, white pepper, cream and parmesan cheese. Add scallops and sauté 3-4 minutes. Add artichoke hearts and sauté 1-2 minutes and then add clams. Drain linguine and add to sauce. Sauté and blend thoroughly, stirring about 2-3 minutes. Serve hot with a dry white wine. Yield: 6 servings

Tomato Walnut Basil Pasta

Ingredients:

One 28oz can crushed tomatoes
2 tbsp extra virgin olive oil
1/2 medium red onion, diced (yield: 1 cup diced)
3 garlic cloves, minced
1 tsp dried oregano
Pinch red pepper flakes
1/2 cup packed fresh basil leaves, stems removed &chopped finely
1 tsp kosher salt, or to taste
Freshly ground black pepper, to taste
1/4 cup parmesan cheese
2 large handfuls spinach, roughly chopped
1/2-3/4 cup walnuts, roughly chopped
Pasta of your choice

Directions:

1. Chop onion and garlic. In a large skillet, heat 2 tbsp of olive oil. Add in the onion and cook over low-medium heat for about 5 minutes. Add in the minced garlic and cook on low for another 4-5 minutes until the onion is translucent.

2. Add in the oregano, salt, and black pepper. Stir well. Cook on low for a few minutes. Now add in the 28oz of crushed tomatoes, chopped basil, and parmesan cheese. Stir. Bring to a low boil and then simmer on low for about 5 minutes. Meanwhile, cook your pasta.

3. Stir in the chopped walnuts and the chopped spinach. Cook for about 10 minutes longer on med-low. Serve over pasta and garnish with basil leaves and additional walnuts. Makes about 3.5 cups sauce.

Wild and Spicy
Southwestern Pasta
Ingredients
1 lb. of Penne Pasta, Cooked ala dente' and drained
1 fresh medium eggplant, peeled and diced
1 red bell pepper, cleaned and diced
1 green bell pepper, cleaned and diced
1 small red onion, peeled and diced
4 tablespoons extra virgin olive oil
2 tablespoon minced garlic
1 small jar Smoked eggplant pesto
1 Jar Green chili stew "505"
¼ lb. Green Chili chicken sausage
8 each peeled, cleaned (tail off) shrimp 26/30 ct.
1 Fresh lime
5 pitted Kalamata olives
10 assorted colored flavored corn chips
Directions: In large pan, cook off pasta and drain with cold water, cover and set aside. N large skillet add the olive oil and garlic heat then add the diced eggplant, bell peppers and onions. Cook for 15 to 20 minutes until the eggplant is soft and tender. Add the pesto and green chili stew, heat then add the chicken sausage and shrimp, cook until the shrimp is pink and tender. Add the pasta to the skillet, toss until pasta is hot, serve this dish in a large bowl, garnish with a squeeze of lime, top with Kalamata olives and surround the dish with assorted flavored corn chips. Serves 4 to 6

Poached Salmon over Pesto Pasta
Ingredients
Pasta 2 cups dry.
Salmon Fillet
4 oz salmon fillet
2 cups of water
1 Tablespoon of lemon juice
½ teaspoon capers
2 Lemon twist
½ teaspoon of dill
Directions: Cook pasta per package directions.
Your choice of pasta (bowtie, penne or rigatoni).
Cook pasta, rinse and drain with cold water, keep in Refrigerator until later use. In large skillet heat water and lemon juice add salmon, cook until salmon is tender and very pink. Keep hot.
Final Touch: In large non-stick skillet, add Pesto sauce, pasta then heat. Place pasta in center of plate top with cooked salmon, sprinkle with capers and garnish with lemon twist.

Pesto Sauce
Ingredients
5 garlic gloves, finely chopped
1/3 cup pine nuts, coarsely chopped
1 teaspoon salt
1/2 cup (2 ounces) grated Romano cheese
1 cup (4 ounces) grated Parmesan cheese
2 cups packed, chopped fresh basil leaves
1/8 teaspoon white pepper
1 cup olive oil
Directions: Easy, using a blender adds all ingredients and blend together, not creamy, just a rough cut.

Veal Picatta
Ingredients
8 ounces veal scaloppini
3 teaspoons olive oil
1 cup Diced tomato's
1 ounce au jus
(Make with beef base as provided to taste)
2 lemon halves
1/3 Cup Marsala wine
1 tablespoon chopped shallots
15-20 capers
Directions: Place veal between parchment paper and pound veal until 1/8" thick. Heat the olive oil in a large, Teflon-coated skillet. Add the Diced tomatoes and au jus, and veal. Cook the veal for 2 minutes on each side and then add the lemon (squeeze lightly before adding), wine, shallots and capers. Yield: 2 serving

New Year's Day Pancakes, Italian Style
Ingredients
For the topping:
12 thin slices prosciutto
4 Golden Delicious apples
1/2 stick butter, melted
1/4 cup maple syrup
For the pancakes:
2 cups ricotta
4 large eggs, separated
1 cup buttermilk
1 tablespoon lemon juice
1 teaspoon lemon zest
1 cup all-purpose flour
3 tablespoons sugar
1 teaspoon baking powder

Pinch salt, Butter, for cooking, Confectioners' sugar, for dusting, optional 1 cup maple syrup, warmed on stove-top

Directions: For the topping:

Preheat oven to 400 degrees F.

On 1 tray lay the slices of prosciutto out in a single flat layer. Season with some salt and freshly ground black pepper, if desired, and pop into the oven. Roast the prosciutto until crispy, about 10 to 15 minutes.

Cut each apple into thirds, remove the cheeks and discard the core. Slice each piece into 4 and toss with butter and maple syrup in a large bowl. Transfer to a roasting pan and place in the oven. Roast the apples until they are fork-tender and slightly caramelized on the top, about 30 to 45 minutes depending on ripeness of the fruit.

For the pancakes:

Combine the ricotta, egg yolks, buttermilk, lemon juice, and lemon zest in a large mixing bowl. Sift the dry ingredients: flour, sugar, baking powder, and salt together into the ricotta mixture and stir until fully combined. In a separate bowl whisk the egg whites until stiff peaks form and then gently fold into the batter.

Heat a large nonstick pan over medium heat and add a little butter. Cook 2 to 3 pancakes at a time using a 6-ounce ladle or measuring cup to pour the batter into the pan. The trick to perfect round pancakes to carefully pour all the batter in the same spot and let it roll out to a complete circle. Cook the pancakes on 1 side until they set. When small bubbles appear on the uncooked surface, flip the pancakes and cook until golden on both sides, about 6 minutes. Keep the pancakes on a plate set at the back of the stove under a dry towel to keep warm while you make the rest. To serve, lay the pancakes on a plate and dust with confectioners' sugar. Serve with roasted apples, crispy prosciutto strips and warm maple syrup.

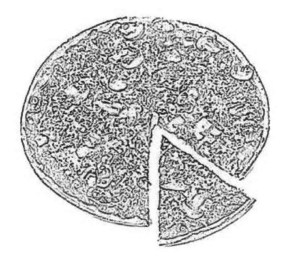

Aunt "Babe's" Spinach Pizza Pie
Traditional Pizza Dough Recipe
Ingredients:
1 envelope of dry yeast
1/4 teaspoon of sugar
3/4 cup of lukewarm water
1 3/4 cups of unbleached plain flour
1/2 teaspoon of salt
Directions: Combine 1 envelope of dry yeast, 1/4 teaspoon of sugar
and 3/4 cups of lukewarm water. Mix a little and let sit for 6-8 minutes.
Combine 1 3/4 cups of unbleached plain flour with 1/2 teaspoon of salt
in a bowl or food processor. Pour the water combination into the bowl
(or food processor) and mix until ready to knead (around 30 second in
a food processor). If using a bowl, mix with a spoon until you have a
neat ball.

Pizza Sauce 1

Ingredients:

1 **Basic pizza dough recipe**

1 28 oz. can of crushed tomatoes

1/2 cup extra virgin olive oil plus 1 tablespoon

1 medium onion, chopped

2 tbsps. minced fresh garlic

1 t. dried oregano

1 t. dried basil

4 tbsps. Pecorino Romano

1 t dried parsley

1 t sugar

Spinach and Cheese

2 8oz package of frozen chopped spinach, thawed and drained

1/2 pound Low fat mozzarella cheese

Directions: Preheat the oven to 425°F. Whisk all the sauce ingredients together. Allow flavors to blend for one hour before using.

Prepare a lightly sprinkled surface with flour. Roll out the dough to an eighth of an inch thick and lay it in a lightly oiled pizza pan.

Using the tomato sauce and all the cheese, cover the pizza, and then place the spinach over the entire pizza. Cover the pizza with a top layer of dough, pinch the side together and brush with olive oil. Bake in your preheated oven 425F for 20 minutes or until crisp (times may vary based on different ovens). Serve immediately.

Pizza Sauce 2

This recipe was developed for the best tasting pizza in the world

Ingredients

1 1 pound can of tomato puree

½ tablespoon sweet basil

½ tablespoon chopped oregano

½ tablespoon garlic powder

½ tablespoon ground black pepper

¼ cup Worcestershire sauce
3 dashes Tabasco sauce
1/3 cup sugar
Salt to taste

Directions: Empty tomato puree in mixing bowl. Add all spices including Worcestershire sauce and sugar. Mix very well. Cover pizza lightly with sauce and add your favorite topping. I can give you many recipes for dough, however to make it easier my Mother started using frozen raw dough and for home this is the easiest. They come 3 loafs per package. Let them thaw; I rub a little olive oil on the top and place in the refrigerator for 24 hours. Once thawed using flour and a rolling pin roll out to the thickness you like. I prefer then, Valery prefers a little thinker. So I usually make 4 or 5 pizza out of the three loafs. Pre heat your oven to 500 degrees, use a pizza pan and with a fork perforate the dough. Place a little sauce then very little cheese on top of each pizza. Add the topping you like then add a little more cheese. I use three cheese, shredded low fat mozzarella, jack and cheddar. In Italy they make very thin crust with very little cheese. Be creative and I always let the kids pick what they wanted. It took no more effort to make three different individual pizzas, and it avoid lots of fights! To make a Calzone just roll out the dough about 10inchs add your sauce and filling, fold, using a fork press on all sides and bake just like the pizza.

Slow Cooker Beef Barbacoa
Ingredients
½ to 2 Lbs beef brisket
2 cup can diced tomatoes with juice
1 cup chicken broth
¼ cup red wine
2 tablespoons lime juice
1 ½ Teaspoon dried ground cumin
1 teaspoon dried ground oregano
1 sliced and deseeded jalapeno
3 tablespoons cilantro
1 large thickly sliced onions
½ teaspoon salt
½ teaspoon pepper
2 Tablespoons olive oil
Directions
Combine all ingredients in a Ziploc bag. Marinate meat in all ingredients overnight or at least for 4 hours in refrigerator; turn bag over at least once while marinating. These ingredients can be frozen but needs to be completely thawed before cooking. Heat 2 tablespoon of the olive oil in a large heavy skillet over medium-high heat. Brown the brisket well on all sides, making meat caramelized but still raw in the middle. Place the browned meat in crock-pot. Combine all marinated ingredients from bag in to the Crock-pot; cover and cook for 8 hours on LOW or 5 to 6 hours on HIGH, or until the meat is fork-tender and can be easily shred with a fork. Service on tortillas, with graded cheese, guacamole, salsa and sour cream.

Beef and Bean Chimichangas
Ingredients:
1 pound lean ground beef
3/4 cup chopped onion
3/4 cup diced green bell pepper
1 1/2 cups whole kernel corn
2 cups taco sauce
2 teaspoons chili powder
1 teaspoon garlic salt
1 teaspoon ground cumin
1 (16 ounce) can refried beans
8 (12 inch) flour tortillas
1 (16 ounce) package shredded
Monterey Jack cheese
1 tablespoon butter, melted
shredded lettuce
1 tomato, diced
Directions: Preheat the oven to 350 degrees F (175 degrees C).
Brown the ground beef in a skillet over medium-high heat.
Drain excess grease, and add the onion, bell pepper, and corn.
Cook for about 5 more minutes, or until vegetables are tender.
Stir in the taco sauce, and season with chili powder, garlic salt
and cumin, stirring until blended. Cook until heated through,
then remove from heat, and set aside.
Open the can of beans, and spread a thin layer of beans onto
each of the tortillas. Spoon the beef mixture down the center,
and then top with as much shredded cheese as you like.
Roll up the tortillas, and place them seam-side down onto a
baking sheet. Brush the tortillas with melted butter.
Bake for 30 to 35 minutes in the preheated oven, or until golden brown.
Serve with lettuce and tomato.

Indian Tacos

Ingredients:

Topping:

1 pound ground beef

1 (1.25 ounce) package taco seasoning
mix

1 (15.5 ounce) can pinto beans, with
liquid

1 cup shredded Cheddar cheese

2 cups shredded iceberg lettuce

1/2 cup picante sauce

FRY BREAD:

2 cups all-purpose flour

1 tablespoon baking powder

1 teaspoon salt

1 cup milk

4 cups oil for frying, or as needed

Directions: Combine beans and 2 tablespoons of picante sauce
in a small saucepan over low heat. Cook until heated through.
In a large skillet, over medium-high heat, cook the ground beef
with taco seasoning mix according to seasoning mix package
directions. Cover, and keep warm while you prepare the fry bread.
In a medium bowl, stir together the flour, baking powder,
and salt. Stir In milk, and mix until the dough comes together.
Add more flour if necessary to be able to handle the dough.
On a floured surface, knead the dough until smooth, at least 5 minutes.
Let the dough rest for 5 minutes.
Heat oil in a large, deep heavy skillet to 365 degrees F (180 degrees C).
Oil should be about 1 1/2 inches deep. Break off 3/4 cup sized
pieces of dough, and shape into round discs 1/4 inch in thickness,
making a thinner depressed area in the center. Fry breads in the
hot oil until golden on both sides, turning only once. Drain on paper
towels. Top fry bread with beans, ground beef, lettuce and cheese.

Spoon picante sauce over. You can also top with other of your favorite taco toppings, such as onion, sour cream or guacamole

Chile Rellenos
Ingredients
12 Poblano chile peppers, seeded and membranes removed.
3/4 lbs Cheddar cheese
1 cup milk
1 egg, beaten
1 cup all-purpose flour
1 tsp baking powder
1 tsp baking soda
1 tsp salt
1/2 cup all-purpose flour
1 tsp ground cumin
1 tsp canola oil
Directions
De-seed and membrane the peppers and quickly char on high heat on the grill (turn multiple times while charring). Set aside. In a medium bowl, mix milk, egg, 1 cup flour, baking powder, baking soda, salt, and oil.
Slice your cheese into strips (1/2 inch thick) and sprinkle with cumin. Place 1-2 strips of cheese inside each pepper. Heat (on medium) a heavy bottom fry pan and pour enough oil to cover about 1" of the pan. While heating, dust the peppers with remaining flour (1/2 cup), and dip into milk / egg mix.
When hot, fry your peppers 3-4 at a time for about 4-5 minutes on each side. Should turn a nice brown. Serve hot!

Chile Relleno Casserole
Ingredients
1 lb grated cheese (i use a Mexican blend or a cheddar also works well)
3 eggs
1 1/2 cups milk
1/2 cup flour
6 Poblano chilies - roasted and peeled
Directions: Mix the milk, eggs, salt, pepper, and flour. Spray a pan (9x13) with a nonstick cooking spray. layer chilies, then the mixture made in step 1, then the cheese. Continue this order until you run out of ingredients and put EXTRA cheese on the top! Bake at 350 degrees for about 50 minutes. Allow about 10 minutes before serving!

Enchilada Pie
Great dish for pot lucks
Ingredients
2 pounds lean ground round
8 ounces freshly shredded cheddar cheese
2 small cans chopped black olives
1 small diced red onion
2 pints sour cream
2 8 ounce cans mild enchilada sauce
1 8 ounce can hot enchilada sauce
2 dozen corn tortillas
Directions: Preheat oven to 350 F. Cook hamburger well, drain and place in a large bowl. Add 6 ounces of cheese, olives, onions and sour cream. Mix together well. Place enchilada sauces in sauce pan, mix well and warm. Dip corn tortillas in warmed sauce and place in a baking pan to cover bottom of pan. Add 1/2 the hamburger mixture to top of tortillas and spread evenly to cover. Add small amount of sauce and spread to cover. Place second layer of tortillas and remainder of hamburger mixture on top of the first layer. Cover with small amount of sauce. Add final layer of tortillas and cover with sauce and

remainder of cheese. Bake for 30 minutes.
Yield: 8 - 10 servings

Fajitas
Ingredients
1 1/2 pounds skirt steak
1 green or red bell pepper, cored, seeded, and thinly sliced
1 small onion, thinly sliced
3 tomatoes, chopped
Shredded Cheddar cheese
Salsa & Flour tortillas
Directions: Prepare Lime Marinade. Lay the skirt steak on a cutting
board and remove the outer membrane (grab the membrane with one
hand and slide the knife beneath it, cutting as you go). Using a sharp
paring knife, make a number of slits in the meat, cutting both with and
against the grain of the meat (this cuts the muscle fiber and reduces
any toughness.)

In a large plastic bag with Lim Marinade, add skirt steak; reseal and
marinate in the refrigerator at least 1 hour or overnight, turning steak
occasionally. Remove steak from refrigerator and bring to room
temperature before cooking. Preheat barbecue. Drain steaks, reserving
marinade. Place steak on hot grill and spoon some of the reserved
marinade onto the steak. Close barbecue lid, open any vents, and cook
3 to 5 minutes for medium-rare. Remove from grill and transfer to a
cutting board; cut on the diagonal into thin strips.

Preheat oven to 350 degrees F. Wrap stacked tortillas in aluminum foil
and heat in oven 15 minutes or until hot. To microwave, wrap a stack
of tortillas lightly in paper towels and warm on high for 6 or 7 seconds
per tortilla.

When the shirt steak is cooking, grill the green pepper and onion slices 1 to 2 minutes or until soft; remove from grill and place on a serving platter. Place cooked steak strips onto the same platter. For each fajita, fill a warm tortilla with cooked steak and desired amounts of green pepper and onion slices. Add tomatoes, Cheddar cheese, and salsa as desired; roll up like a burrito and enjoy.

Lime Marinade
Ingredients
Juice of 4 to 5 limes
1/4 cup red wine vinegar
1 tablespoon soy sauce
1 tablespoon light molasses
1 tablespoon chopped fresh cilantro leaves
2 cloves garlic, minced
1/2 teaspoon ground cumin
1/2 teaspoon black pepper
Directions: In a large resalable plastic bag, combine lime juice, vinegar, soy sauce, molasses, cilantro, garlic, cumin, and pepper; set aside

Mexican Salad Roll up
Ingredients
1 lg. head lettuce, chopped
2 or 3 tomatoes, chopped
1 bell pepper, chopped
1 onion, chopped
1 cup sliced black olives
1 lg. can ranch-style beans (kidney, chili or Mexican beans), rinsed well
1 bottle Catalina French dressing
1 to 1 1/2 lbs. Cheddar cheese, grated
1 lg. bag corn chips, crushed
4 Flour Tortillas

Directions: This salad may be mixed and serve immediately, or prepared using the following method the day before, then mixed together just before serving: Toss together first 4 ingredients. Cover and refrigerate until needed. Mix remaining ingredients when ready to serve. Place salad in tortilla, roll and serve with your favorite salsa the dough should not stick to the sides of the bowl and should cleanly roll in your hands. This can be somewhat of an art, and with practice you will recognize the right consistency. Let the dough "rest" covered in the refrigerator for 30 minutes.

Taco Beef and Noodle Skillet

Ingredients:
1 lb. lean ground beef
1 pkg. Taco Seasoning Mix
2 cups water
1 pkg. Macaroni & Cheese Dinner
1/3 cup low fat sour cream
1 large tomato
1 cup lettuce
1 cup tortilla chips

Directions:
Brown meat in large nonstick skillet on medium-high heat; drain. Add seasoning mix, water and Macaroni; mix well. Bring to boil; cover. Simmer on medium-low heat 7 min. or until macaroni is tender and most of the liquid is absorbed. Add sour cream and Cheese Sauce Mix; mix well.
Top with remaining ingredients.

Tamale Pie Casserole

Ingredients:

1 pound lean ground beef

1 cup chopped onion

1 large green bell pepper, chopped

1 large can (15 ounces) tomato sauce

1 large can (28 ounces) tomatoes, cut up

1 can (16 ounces) whole kernel corn, drained

1 small can (4 ounces) sliced ripe olives

2 cloves garlic, minced

1 tablespoon sugar

1/2 teaspoon salt

2 teaspoons chili powder

dash black pepper

1 cup grated Cheddar or Mexican blend cheese

Crust:

3/4 cup yellow cornmeal

1/2 teaspoon salt

2 cups cold water

1/2 teaspoon chili powder

1 tablespoon butter or margarine

1/2 cup grated Cheddar or Mexican blend cheese, for topping (optional)

Directions: Brown ground beef with onions and green pepper; drain well. Add tomato sauce, tomatoes, corn, olives, garlic, sugar, salt, chili powder and black pepper. Heat to boiling; reduce heat and simmer, uncovered, for about 20 minutes, or until thickened. Add cheese; stir until cheese is melted. Set filling aside. In a saucepan, combine cornmeal, salt, water and chili powder. Cook over medium heat, stirring constantly, until thick. Stir in butter. Spread half of the mixture into a baking dish, about 12- x 8-inches. Spoon filling over bottom crust; spoon remaining cornmeal mixture over filling. Bake at 375° for 45 minutes.

Chicken Lettuce Wraps
Ingredients
1 ts cornstarch
2 ts dry sherry
2 ts water
1 ts soy sauce
Salt and pepper
1 1/2 lb boneless, skinless chicken (diced very small)
5 tb Stir Fry oil
1 tsp fresh minced ginger
2 cloves garlic, minced
2 green onions, minced
2 sm dried chilis
8 oz can bamboo shoots, minced
8 oz can water chestnuts, minced
1 pkg cellophane Chinese rice noodles, prepared according to instructions on pkg.
Cooking sauce:
1 tb hoisin sauce
1 tb soy sauce
1 tb dry sherry
2 tb oyster sauce
2 tb water
1 tsp. sesame oil
1 tsp. sugar
2 tsp. cornstarch

Directions: Iceberg lettuce 'cups' leaves.. Mix all ingredients for cooking sauce in bowl, and set aside. In medium bowl, combine cornstarch, sherry water, soy sauce, salt, pepper, and chicken. Stir to coat chicken thoroughly. Stir in 1 tsp. oil and let sit 15 minutes to marinate. Heat wok or large skillet over medium high heat. Add 3 Tbsp oil, then add chicken and stir fry for about 3-4 minutes. Set aside. Add 2 Tbsp oil to pan. Add ginger, garlic, chilies (if desired), and onion; stir fry about a minute or so. Add bamboo shoots and water chestnuts; stir fry an additional 2 minutes. Return chicken to pan. Add mixed cooking sauce to pan. Cook until thickened and hot. Break cooked cellophane noodles into small pieces, and cover bottom of serving dish with them. Then pour chicken mixture on top of noodles. Spoon into lettuce leaf and Roll.

Chicken Lettuce Wraps for Kids
Ingredients
1 ts cornstarch
2 ts water
1 ts soy sauce
Salt and pepper
1 1/2 lb boneless, skinless chicken (diced very small)
5 tb Stir Fry oil
1 tsp fresh minced ginger
1 cloves garlic, minced
1 green onions, minced
8 oz can bamboo shoots, minced
8 oz can water chestnuts, minced
1 pkg cellophane Chinese rice noodles, prepared according to instructions on pkg.
Cooking sauce:
1 tb Black Bean sauce
1 tb soy sauce
2 tb water

1 tsp. sesame oil
1 tsp. sugar
2 tsp. cornstarch
Directions: Iceberg lettuce 'cups' leaves.. Mix all ingredients for cooking sauce in bowl, and set aside. In medium bowl, combine cornstarch, water, soy sauce, salt, pepper, and chicken. Stir to coat chicken thoroughly. Stir in 1 tsp. oil and let sit 15 minutes to marinate. Heat wok or large skillet over medium high heat. Add 3 Tbsp oil, then add chicken and stir fry for about 3-4 minutes. Add 2 Tbsp oil to pan. Add ginger, garlic, and onion; stir fry about a minute or so. Add Black Bean sauce mix well. Add bamboo shoots and water chestnuts; stir fry an additional 2 minutes. Return chicken to pan. Add mixed cooking sauce to pan. Cook until thickened and hot. Break cooked cellophane noodles into small pieces, and cover bottom of serving dish with them. Then pour chicken mixture on top of noodles. Spoon into lettuce leaf and Roll

Kalua Pork
Ingredients:
4-5 pound pork butt
2½ tablespoons Hawaiian salt (substitute kosher salt)
2 tablespoons liquid smoke
1 banana leaf (substitute 4-5 whole, unpeeled bananas)
4-6 ti leaves (substitute aluminum foil)
Directions: To Make Marinade: Combine 1 tablespoon wine, 1 tablespoon soy sauce, 1 tablespoon oil and 1 tablespoon cornstarch/water mixture and mix together. Place chicken pieces in a glass dish or bowl and add marinade. Toss to coat. Cover dish and place in refrigerator for about 30 minutes.
Trim any excess fat from the roast. Make several shallow long cuts along the roast or pierce liberally with a fork. (This allows the salt and liquid smoke to penetrate the meat.) Rub with salt and liquid smoke. Wrap the roast with banana leaf, than wrap in foil.

Roast in a 250-300 degree oven or BBQ for about 2-3 hours depending on the size. Just figure 45 - 30 minutes per pound. When meat is done, remove foil & banana leaf shred pork.

To Make Sauce: In a small bowl combine 1 tablespoon wine, 1 tablespoon soy sauce, 1 tablespoon oil, 1 tablespoon cornstarch/water mixture, chili paste, vinegar and sugar. Mix together and add green onion, garlic, water chestnuts and peanuts. In a medium skillet, heat sauce slowly until aromatic.

Meanwhile, remove chicken from marinade and saute in a large skillet until meat is white and juices run clear. When sauce is aromatic, add sauteed chicken to it and let simmer together until sauce thickens.

Pork Pot Stickers with Honey Chipotle Sauce
Ingredients:
Sauce:
1 Cup Honey
4 Whole Chipotle Chilies In Adobo Sauce, Minced
2 Tbsp. Adobo Sauce
Pot Stickers:
1 Lb. Lean Ground Pork
1/3 Cup Bamboo Shoots, Minced
4 Medium Scallions, Thinly Sliced (1/4 cup)
1 Tbsp. Dry White Wine or Nonalcoholic Wine
1 Tbsp. Water
1 Tsp. Cornstarch
1 Tsp. Salt
1 Tsp. Sesame Oil
1 Dash Ground White Pepper
2 Cup All Purpose Flour
1 Cup Boiling Water
1/2 Cup Vegetable Oil
2 Cups Water

Directions

Prepare Sauce:

In small bowl, combine honey, chipotle chilies and adobo sauce; set aside.

Prepare Filling: In large bowl, mix pork, bamboo shoots, green onions, wine, 1 tablespoon water, the cornstarch, salt, sesame oil and white pepper.

Prepare Dough:

In medium bowl, mix flour and 1 cup boiling water until a soft dough forms. Knead dough on lightly floured surface about 5 minutes or until smooth. Divide dough in half. Shape each half into a 12-inch-long roll; cut each roll into 24 slices, each about 1/2 inch thick. Roll 1 slice of dough into a 3-inch circle on lightly floured surface. (If the circle springs back, cover the slices with a towel and let rest about 10 minutes or until slice is easy to roll and stays in a circle.) Pot-Sticker Construction: Place 1 tablespoon pork mixture on center of circle. Pinch 5 pleats on edge of one half of circle. Fold circle in half, pressing pleated edge to unpleated edge. (Or instead of pleating the edge, you can fold the circle in half and press edges together with a fork.) Place the dumpling, pleated edge up, on cookie sheet. Gently press dumpling to flatten the bottom. Repeat with remaining slices of dough. Heat wok until very hot. Add 2 tablespoons of the vegetable oil; tilt wok to coat side. Place about 12 dumplings in single layer in wok; fry 2 minutes or until bottoms are golden brown. Add 1/2 cup of the water. Cover and cook 6 to 7 minutes or until water is absorbed. Repeat with remaining dumplings. (Add vegetable oil as necessary.) Serve with sauce.

Thai Chicken Wraps
Thai Peanut Sauce
Ingredients
1 cup sour cream
1/3 cup milk
2 tablespoons Creamy peanut butter
1 teaspoon sesame oil
Mix all ingredients together very well until smooth.
Chicken Filling
Ingredients
1 tablespoon vegetable oil
1 pound chicken breasts boneless, skinless, cut into 1" pieces
1 teaspoon fresh ginger root, minced
3 cups cabbage, shredded
1 1/2 cups carrots, julienne
1/2 cup red pepper flakes
1/4 cup green onion, diced
2/3 cup creamy peanut butter
1/2 cup water
1 tablespoon sesame oil
6 flour tortillas (10 inch) (I prefer the flavored ones)
Directions: In small bowl, combine all sauce ingredients. Cover; refrigerate until serving time. In 10 inch skillet, heat oil until sizzling; stir in chicken and ginger. Cook over medium-high heat until chicken is no longer pink (7 to 9 minutes). Add cabbage, carrots, red pepper and onion; continue cooking until vegetables are crisply tender (5 to 7 minutes). Meanwhile, in 1 quart saucepan, combine peanut butter, water, curry powder and oil. Cook over medium-high heat until mixture is heated through (5 to 7 minutes). Remove from heat add the cooked chicken. Heat Tortilla on hot flat skillet. At serving time, place 1 cup filling in center of each warm tortilla. Fold two opposite edges of tortilla toward center of filling. Roll up open end of tortilla toward opposite edge. Place, seam-side down, on microwave-safe plate. Serve

wrap immediately with sauce for dipping. Makes 6 wraps.

Honey Chicken Wrap Marinade

Directions: Sauté strips of chicken with blueberries, strawberries, raspberries, soy sauce and black pepper. Combine sautéed chicken mixture with the filler below and put in a honey wrap. Filler - Mandarin oranges (cold) Lettuce (shredded), Cottage cheese

Pad Thai

Ingrediants:

1 (12 ounce) package rice noodles

2 tablespoons butter

1 pound boneless, skinless chicken breast halves, cut into bite-sized pieces

1/4 cup vegetable oil

4 eggs

1 tablespoon white wine vinegar

2 tablespoons fish sauce

3 tablespoons white sugar

1/8 tablespoon crushed red pepper

2 cups bean sprouts

1/4 cup crushed peanuts

3 green onions, chopped

1 lemon, cut into wedges

Directions:

Soak rice noodles in cold water 30 to 50 minutes, or until soft. Drain, and set aside.

Heat butter in a wok or large heavy skillet. Saute chicken until browned. Remove, and set aside. Heat oil in wok over medium-high heat. Crack eggs into hot oil, and cook until firm. Stir in chicken, and cook for 5 minutes. Add softened noodles, and vinegar, fish sauce, sugar and red pepper. Adjust seasonings to taste. Mix while cooking, until noodles are tender. Add bean sprouts, and mix for 3 minutes.

Pho Bo Soup - Vietnamese Beef Noodle Soup
Ingredients:
Beef Broth:
1 small onion, chopped
1 2-inch stick ginger
2 pounds beef bones
12 cups water
6 star anise
1 teaspoon salt
1 teaspoon sugar
1 pound lean, tender beef
Noodles:
1 16-ounce package dry, flat rice noodles (pho)
Garnish:
3 scallions, thinly sliced
1 large onion, thinly sliced
10 cilantro sprigs, finely chopped
1 cup bean sprouts
10 sprigs basil
10 sprigs fresh cilantro (ngo gai)
fresh red or green chili pepper, thinly sliced
Accompaniments
lime or lemon quarters
fish sauce
hoisin sauce
hot chili sauce

Directions:
Broil onion and ginger until they look burned. Using back of cleaver, smash the ginger and set aside.

Wash beef bones, place in a large soup pot and add water to cover. Bring to a boil and immediately pour off this "first boiling" water and discard. Add another 12 cups of fresh water and again bring to a boil. Skim off foam. Add the broiled onion and ginger, star anise, salt and sugar. Over medium-low heat, simmer for 30 minutes. Slice raw beef into thin strips and set aside.

Remove bones from broth and strain out vegetables and seasonings. Soak noodles in cold water for 10 minutes. Drain. In a soup pot bring two quarts fresh water to a boil. Add drained noodles and cook seven minutes at a rolling boil, stirring occasionally until noodles are tender. Rinse noodles under cold running water and set aside.

Return the broth to a boil over high heat.

To serve: Divide noodles among 4 to 6 large individual serving bowls. Arrange thinly sliced raw beef, scallions, onion, and cilantro on top. Pour boiling hot broth to cover noodles and serve immediately. The boiling broth will cook the thin slices of beef. Pho is always accompanied by bean sprouts, basil leaves, cilantro and chili pepper. Serve with lime and lemon quarters, fish sauce, hoisin sauce and hot chili sauce. Serves 4 to 6.

Honey-Soy Broiled Salmon

Ingredients

1 scallion, minced

2 tablespoons reduced-sodium soy sauce

1 tablespoon rice vinegar

1 tablespoon honey

1 teaspoon minced fresh ginger

1 pound center-cut salmon fillet, skinned (see Tip) and cut into 4 portions

1 teaspoon toasted sesame seeds, (see Tip)

Directions:

Whisk scallion, soy sauce, vinegar, honey and ginger in a medium bowl until the honey is dissolved. Place salmon in a sealable plastic bag, add 3 tablespoons of the sauce and refrigerate; let marinate for 15 minutes. Reserve the remaining sauce.

Preheat broiler. Line a small baking pan with foil and coat with cooking spray.

Transfer the salmon to the pan, skinned-side down. (Discard the marinade.) Broil the salmon 4 to 6 inches from the heat source until cooked through, 6 to 10 minutes. Drizzle with the reserved sauce and garnish with sesame seeds. 4 servings

Tangelo Pork Stir-Fry
Ingredients
2 tangelos, such as Minneolas or Honeybells
3 teaspoons toasted sesame oil, divided
1 pound pork tenderloin, trimmed and cut into thin strips
2 medium shallots, thinly sliced
2 cloves garlic, minced
2 tablespoons minced fresh ginger
1/4 teaspoon crushed red pepper
2 red bell peppers, thinly sliced
2 stalks celery, thinly sliced
2 tablespoons reduced-sodium soy sauce
1 tablespoon rice vinegar
2 teaspoons cornstarch
Directions:
Using a vegetable peeler, remove zest from tangelos in long strips. Cut the strips lengthwise into very thin pieces. Cut the tangelos in half and squeeze enough juice from them to get 1/2 cup.
Heat a large wok or skillet over medium-high heat. Swirl in 2 teaspoons oil, then add pork and cook, stirring, until just cooked, 2 to 3 minutes. Transfer to a plate.
Add the remaining 1 teaspoon oil to the pan along with shallots, garlic, ginger, crushed red pepper and the zest. Cook, stirring, for 1 minute. Add bell peppers and celery and cook, stirring constantly, until crisp-tender, about 2 minutes. Stir in the tangelo juice and soy sauce; bring to a simmer. Cook for 1 minute.

Whisk vinegar and cornstarch in a small bowl, then pour it into the pan along with the pork and its juices. Cook, stirring often, until thickened and bubbling and the pork is heated through, about 1 minute. 4 servings

Vegetables and Side Dishes
Apple Stuffing
Ingredients
4 tablespoons bacon fat
3 cups diced, unpeeled tart apples
3 teaspoons sugar
1 box cornbread dressing mix
1/4 tablespoon nutmeg
1/4 teaspoon cinnamon
2 cups chicken broth
1/2 cup Marsala wine
Directions: Melt the bacon fat in a skillet. Add the apples and sugar.

Cook, stirring, over medium low heat for 5 minutes. Remove from heat and toss in remaining ingredients. Dressing should be moist. If you are going to cook the stuffing in the turkey, stuff the turkey just before placing it in the oven; be sure to remove all of the stuffing before serving. If you are cooking the stuffing separately, place stuffing in a 2 inch deep baking dish, cover, and bake in a preheated 350 degree oven for 20 minutes. Yield: 10 - 12 servings

Baked Stuffed Artichokes
Ingredients
4 each large artichokes
1/3 cup lemon juice
1/3 cup Olive oil
½ cup Italian style bread crumbs
1/3 cup Parmesan cheese
Directions: Cut top tips off artichokes, cut ¼ inch off steam. Place artichokes in boiling water cook for 90 minutes or until bottom leaves pull off easily. Remove from water cut in half. Place breadcrumbs between leaves and top with Parmesan cheese. Place artichokes on baking sheet pan and sprinkle with olive oil and bake for 30 minutes. 4 serving Serve hot

Barbequed Beans
Ingredients
1   16 ounce can pork and beans
1/2 cup barbeque sauce (prefer Bull's Eye Original)
1/4 cup dark brown sugar
1/4 cup chopped red onion
1/4 cup chopped green bell pepper
Directions: Preheat oven to 350 F. Open canned beans, drain and place in oven-safe baking dish. Add barbeque sauce, sugar, onions and bell pepper and mix well. Cover with foil and bake for 45 minutes until hot. Yield: 20 servings

Black-Eyed Peas
It's good luck to eat black-eyed peas on New Year's Day
Ingredients
1-2 bags black-eyed peas
1 pound sausage or ham hocks
1-1/2 cups chopped red onion
1/2 cup chopped scallions
2/3 cup chopped green bell peppers
1/3 cup chopped celery
3 tablespoons minced dried parsley
2 teaspoons minced garlic
3/4 teaspoon black pepper
1/8 teaspoon cayenne pepper
1/2 teaspoon ground thyme
1/2 teaspoon ground basil
1/4 teaspoon ground marjoram
1/8 teaspoon ground mace
1 quart cold water

Directions: Soak black-eyed peas overnight and drain. In a large stock pot add all the ingredients (if you are using sausage, cook and drain before adding to stock pot). Cook for 1-2 hours or until peas are tender. Serve hot. Yield: 10 servings

Broccoli Cooked in Wine
Ingredients
2 pounds broccoli
5 tablespoons olive oil
1 each garlic clove, finely chopped
Salt and white pepper to taste
1-1/2 cups Marsala wine

Directions: Rinse broccoli under running cold water. Cut broccoli florets from stems; remove any thick stems. Cut a cross into the base of remaining stems for even cooking. Heat oil in a large sauce pan. Add garlic and sauté about 3 minutes. Add broccoli florets. Season with salt and white pepper to taste. Sauté 3 to 4 minutes in hot oil. Stir in wine a little at a time. Cover and simmer for 20 minutes or until broccoli is crisp-tender. Drain. Serve with roasted meats.

Chanukah Latkes
Ingredients
5 large potatoes, peeled
1 large red onion
3 eggs
1/3 cup flour
1 tsp. Kosher Salt
¼ tsp. pepper
¾ cup extra virgin olive oil
Directions: Grate potatoes and onion on the fine side of a grater, or in a food processor. Strain grated potatoes and onion through a colander, pressing out excess water. Place into mixing bowl and add eggs, flour, and seasoning. Mix well. Heat ½ cup oil in 10 inch skillet. Lower flame and place 1 large tablespoon batter at a time into hot sizzling oil and fry on one side for approximately 5 minutes until golden brown. Turnover and fry on other side 2 to 3 minutes. Remove from pan and place on paper towels to drain excess oil. Continue with remaining batter until used up, adding more oil when necessary. Serve with applesauce on the side.

Streamed Onions with Lima Beans

Ingredients

1 10 ounce package frozen lima beans

2 9 ounce packages frozen small onions in cream sauce

1-1/3 cups water

3 tablespoons butter

1/2 teaspoon curry powder

Directions: Cook lima beans in boiling salted water until barely tender; drain. Combine frozen onions with sauce, water, butter and curry powder. Cover and bring to a full boil, lower heat and simmer covered for 4 minutes, stirring occasionally. Remove from heat. Stir just until sauce is smooth. Stir in beans. Return to low heat until beans are hot. Serve hot. Yield: 4 - 6 servings

Golden Hominy

This is a true Southern-style recipe ~ and I don't mean southern Italy

Ingredients

1 pound bacon

2 8 ounce cans yellow hominy

1/2 cup diced green onions

1/4 cup diced pimiento

2 teaspoons salt

2 teaspoons white pepper

2 teaspoons garlic powder

Directions: Cook bacon until crisp and crumble in pan it was cooked in. Without draining pan, add hominy, green onions, pimiento, salt, white pepper and garlic powder to taste. Simmer until hot. Yield: 8 servings

Giblet Gravy

Ingredients

Cooked giblets and neck from turkey

2 cups stock from giblets, chicken base or pan drippings from turkey

3 tablespoons melted butter

3 tablespoons flour

Salt and pepper to taste

Directions: Heat stock to boiling. Dice giblets. Mix flour and butter to make a roux. Slowly add roux to stock, stirring constantly until smooth. Add giblets. Simmer for 10 minutes to develop flavor. Add salt and pepper to taste.

Herbed Potato Pie
Ingredients
10 baking potatoes washed and unpeeled
4 cloves garlic minced
4 shallots chopped
3 T. fresh parsley
1 T. fresh herbs (thyme, rosemary, sage, basil, oregano...pick one)
1 C. asiago cheese
4 T. parmesan cheese
1 C. chicken broth
Salt and freshly ground pepper

Directions: Preheat oven to 350° F. Slice potatoes into 1/8 inch slices. Coat a 12 inch round baking dish with butter. Slightly overlap potato slices in the bottom to form a spiral. Combine asiago cheese, garlic, shallots, parsley, salt and pepper in a small bowl. Sprinkle 1/3 of this mixture over the potatoes. Add two more layers of potatoes and cheese. Pour chicken broth over to cover potatoes. Sprinkle with parmesan cheese. Bake for 45 minutes or until potatoes are tender. Cut into wedges and serve

Heirloom Tomato Pie
Ingredients
1 cup all-purpose flour
3/4 cup yellow cornmeal
3/4 teaspoon fine salt
1 stick cold unsalted butter, cut into 1/2-inch pieces
3/4 cup plus 3 tablespoons shredded parmesan cheese

2 tablespoons extra-virgin olive oil
1 large onion, thinly sliced
2 1/4 pounds mixed heirloom tomatoes
Kosher salt
3/4 cup shredded mozzarella cheese
1/4 cup mayonnaise
3 tablespoons breadcrumbs
3 tablespoons chopped fresh chives
3 tablespoons chopped fresh parsley
Freshly ground pepper

Directions

Make the crust: Pulse the flour, cornmeal and fine salt in a food processor to combine. Add the butter and 3 tablespoons parmesan; pulse until the mixture looks like coarse meal with pea-size bits of butter. Drizzle in 4 tablespoons ice water and pulse until the dough comes together; add 1 more tablespoon ice water if necessary. Turn out onto a sheet of plastic wrap and pat into a disk. Wrap and refrigerate until firm, about 45 minutes.

Put the dough between 2 sheets of parchment paper and roll into a 13-inch round. Transfer the dough to a 9 1/2-inch deep-dish pie plate. Fold the overhang under itself and crimp the edges. Pierce the bottom of the crust all over with a fork. Refrigerate until firm, about 20 minutes. Meanwhile, preheat the oven to 350 degrees F.

Line the crust with foil, then fill with dried beans. Bake until the edges are golden, about 20 minutes. Remove the foil and beans and continue baking until golden all over, 10 to 15 more minutes. Transfer to a rack to cool.

Make the filling: Heat 1 tablespoon olive oil in a large skillet over medium heat. Add the onion and cook, stirring, until golden, about 15 minutes. Let cool. Meanwhile, thinly slice the tomatoes; toss with 1 teaspoon kosher salt in a colander. Let drain, gently tossing occasionally, about 30 minutes.

Increase the oven temperature to 375 degrees F. Combine the remaining 3/4 cup parmesan, the mozzarella, mayonnaise, breadcrumbs, 2 tablespoons each chives and parsley, 1/4 teaspoon each kosher salt and pepper, and the sauteed onion in a bowl. Spread in the crust. Arrange the tomatoes on top. Drizzle with the remaining 1 tablespoon olive oil and season with pepper. Bake until the tomatoes are browned, about 50 minutes. Top with the remaining 1 tablespoon each chives and parsley.

Lemon Sauce
Just a good sauce for chicken or fish.
Ingredients
2 cups lemon juice into pot cooking on a low heat
¼ cup sherry wine into pot
1 teaspoon lemon pepper into pot
1/3 cup granulated sugar into pot
½ teaspoon salt into pot
1 tablespoon honey into pot
½ teaspoon yellow food coloring into pot
Directions: Mix about ½ cup corn starch and water slowly to pot to thicken Yield 2 ¼ cups

Potato Kugel
Moist on the inside and crispy on the outside, is a staple of Eastern European Jewish cooking. While there are many variations of potato kugel (which add carrots, zucchini, garlic...), this Basic Potato Kugel recipe is still my favorite.
Ingredients
8 medium potatoes
2 Red Onions
6 eggs
1/2 cup Extra Virgin Olive Oil
4 Tbsp. all-purpose flour

1 heaping Tbsp. Kosher salt
1/2-1 tsp. pepper
Directions: Preheat oven to 400° F. In a large bowl, mix eggs, oil, flour, salt and pepper. Set aside. Coarsely grate the potatoes and onion by hand or food processor. Let stand 3-5 minutes. Squeeze out excess liquid. Add grated potatoes to the egg-flour mixture. Mix well until smooth. Pour into a greased 9x13 inch baking dish.
Bake, uncovered, for 1 hour or until golden brown on top and a knife inserted in the middle comes out clean. YIELD: 10-12 servings.

Potato Pancakes
Ingredients
2 pounds raw potatoes
1/4 cup chopped white onion
1/4 ounce lemon juice
1/3 tablespoon chopped dried parsley
1 cup flour
1/4 teaspoon ground nutmeg
1 teaspoon salt
1/2 teaspoon black pepper
3 eggs, separated
1/4 cup olive oi
Directions: Peel potatoes and cut into pieces. Place potatoes and onions in a small food processor and grate (do not drain the juice). Add the lemon juice. Place mixture into a bowl and add the parsley, flour, nutmeg, salt, pepper and egg yolks. Beat the egg whites until stiff and gently fold into mixture. Place 1/2 cup portions of mixture on a well-greased griddle and fry. (Note: As you put the batter on the griddle, flatten slightly by tapping with the bottom of a ladle. Turn pancake over when edges start to raise from griddle. Pancake is cooked when edges of other side curl up.) Yield: 10 servings

Potato, Turnip, and Chard Sauté
Ingredients
1 pound red new potatoes
1 pound turnips peeled
1 pound chard
4 tablespoons butter
2 tablespoons minced shallots
1 teaspoon minced garlic
2 tablespoons olive oil
1 teaspoon stone-ground mustard
2 tablespoons sour cream
2 tablespoons lemon juice
Salt and freshly ground pepper to taste
Directions: Boil potatoes in lightly salted water until tender when pierced with a knife. Drain and set aside. Cut large potatoes in halves or quarters; leave small ones whole. Boil turnips in lightly salted water until tender when pierced with a knife. Drain and set aside. Cut large turnips in halves and quarters; leave small ones whole. Cut chard ribs away from leaves. Blanch leaves and ribs separately in lightly salted water, cooking just until tender (3 to 5 minutes). Drain and plunge into ice water to stop the cooking. Drain again. Chop leaves coarsely; dice ribs. In a small skillet over moderately low heat, melt 2 tablespoons butter. Add shallots and garlic and sauté until fragrant (2 to 3 minutes). Set mixture aside. At serving time, in a large skillet warm remaining butter and olive oil over moderately high heat. Add softened shallot-garlic mixture and chard ribs and sauté quickly to heat through. Add potatoes and turnips and sauté quickly to heat through. Add chard leaves and cook 20 seconds. Stir in mustard and sour cream. Add lemon juice and season with salt and pepper. Makes 4 servings.

Risotto
Ingredients
1 cup Arborio rice
1tbsp. Olive oil
1 large onion, chopped
1/4 cup Parmesan cheese, grated
4-5 cups hot chicken stock (or water)
1/2 cup Marsala (optional)
Directions: Heat olive oil in a heavy non-stick 2-quart pot. Sauté onion in oil until translucent. Add rice and stir rice until grains are coated with oil Add Marsala wine and stir constantly on medium heat until wine is absorbed. Add 1 cup hot chicken stock or water, stirring until liquid is absorbed. Continue cooking for about 20 minutes, adding the remaining liquid 1 cup at a time. This rice creates its own creamy sauce. Remove from heat, stir in cheeses and serve immediately. For variety add fresh herbs, chopped vegetables, and sun dried tomato's during the last 5 minutes of cooking.   I always garnish with fresh chopped Basil sprinkled on top.

Spanish Corn
Ingredients
1 large chopped green bell pepper
1 large chopped red bell pepper
1/2 diced red onion
2 tablespoons olive oil
2   15 ounce cans whole kernel corn, drained
1/4 teaspoon salt
1/4 teaspoon white pepper
Directions: In a large skillet, sauté red and green bell peppers and onions in oil. Add corn and mix well. Season with salt and pepper to taste. Serve hot. Yield: 10 servings

Special Rice
Ingredients
2 cups water
3 tablespoons dry chicken base
1 cup uncooked Uncle Ben's converted rice
2 tablespoons olive oil
1 cup diced green bell pepper
1 small diced red onion
1 small jar diced pimientos
1/4 cup bacon bits or ham bits
2 teaspoons chopped dried parsley
1 tablespoon oregano
1 tablespoon minced garlic
Directions: In a large sauce pan, bring water and chicken base to a boil. Add rice and cook until done ~ light and fluffy. Add oil to skillet and sauté bell pepper, onion, pimiento, bacon or ham bits, parsley, oregano and garlic. When rice is cooked, add to skillet and mix well. Serve covered in a double boiler. Yield: 10 servings

Steamed Spinach with Olive Oil and Grarlic
Ingredients:
1 package (2 pounds) frozen cut leaf spinach
2 large garlic cloves, minced
1-1/2 tablespoons olive oil
Salt and pepper to taste
Directions:
Place frozen spinach in a large microwave-safe bowl with lid. Add about 2 tablespoons water. Cover and cook at High heat for 8 to 10 minutes, depending on microwave wattage. Stir occasionally several times while cooking. When hot, drain well.
Place the garlic and olive oil in a small microwave-safe bowl. Cover with a paper towel and cook on High for about 40 seconds or until the garlic is softened, stirring occasionally and making certain the garlic

does not brown. Pour the garlic and oil over the drained spinach. Add salt and pepper to taste. Stir well to combine. Return to microwave and heat for another minute. Serve immediately or cover to keep hot, returning to the microwave for another minute to reheat if necessary. Serves 4 to 6

Sweet Potato Bake
Ingredients
4 medium sweet potatoes peeled and diced
4 T. butter
2 T. heavy cream
1/4 C. brown sugar
2 large eggs well beaten
1/2 C. milk
1 T. vanilla
1 t. cinnamon
Topping:
1 C. brown sugar
1/3 C. flour
1/3 stick butter softened
1 C. chopped pecans
Directions: Preheat the oven to 350° F.
Place the sweet potatoes in a saucepan and cover them with water. Bring to a boil and reduce to heat to medium .Cook for about 20 minutes, until sweet potatoes are tender. Drain well. Place potatoes in a large bowl and mash them with the butter and cream. Whip in the brown sugar, eggs, vanilla, cinnamon and milk. Beat until smooth. Spoon the mixture into a 13 x 9 inch pan. Combine the topping ingredients together in another bowl. Sprinkle the mixture over the sweet potatoes. Bake until brown, about 35 minutes.

Desserts

Aunt Mary's Poppy Seed Cake
She always made the best cakes. She would make a small cake with no nuts for me as she knew I did not like nuts in my cake.
Ingredients:
1 (18.25-ounce) package yellow cake mix
1/2 cup poppy seed
1 (3 5-ounce) package Instant vanilla pudding
1/4 cup powdered sugar
4 large eggs
1 cup sour cream
1 cup vegetable oil
2 teaspoons butter flavoring
1/2 cup sweet sherry

Directions: Preheat oven to 350 F. In a mixer bowl, combine yellow cake mix, instant vanilla pudding mix, eggs, sour cream, and vegetable oil, Butter flavoring, sherry, and poppy seeds. Beat for 5 minutes. Pour batter into a greased fluted cake pan Bake for 1 hour. Cool for 15 minutes before removing from the pan. Sprinkle with powdered sugar.

Aunt Jeans Chocolate Chip Cookies Recipe
Ingredients:
3/4 cup sugar
3/4 cup packed brown sugar
1 cup butter
1 large egg
2 1/4 cups all-purpose flour
1 teaspoon baking soda
1/2 teaspoon salt
2 cups semisweet chocolate chips
If desired, 1 cup chopped pecans
Directions: Preheat oven to 375 degrees. Mix sugar, brown sugar, butter and egg in a large bowl by hand. Stir in flour, baking soda, and salt. The dough will be very stiff. Stir in chocolate chips. Drop dough by rounded tablespoonfuls 2 inches apart onto ungreased cookie sheet. Bake 8 to 10 minutes or until light brown.
The centers will be soft. Let cool for one minute then remove from cookie sheet and place on wire rack to finish cooling.

Easy Baklava
Ingredients
 Safflower oil for coating pan
1 cup ground almonds
1 cup ground walnuts
1 ½ teaspoons cinnamon
8 sheets filo
¼ cup melted unsalted butter

1 ¼ cups date sugar
2 tablespoons grated lemon rind
¼ cup lemon juice
2 tablespoons honey
Directions: Preheat oven to 350 degrees F. Lightly oil a deep 9- by 12-inch baking pan. In a small bowl combine almonds, walnuts, and cinnamon. Set aside. Cut each sheet of filo in half. Stack cut sheets on counter. With a large pastry brush, dot top sheet with about 1 teaspoon butter, then spread evenly to coat as much of sheet as possible. Lay evenly in baking pan. Sprinkle lightly with nut mixture. Repeat with remaining sheets, stacking evenly.

To cut baklava make 4 evenly spaced vertical cuts through the entire stack of filo. Then cut diagonally to form diamond shapes. (Four evenly spaced diagonal cuts with yield 15 to 20 pastries.) Bake for 20 minutes, then lower heat to 300 degrees F and bake for 30 minutes more.

In a small saucepan over medium-high heat, simmer date sugar, lemon rind, lemon juice, and honey until thickened. Pour over cooked baklava as soon as it comes out of the oven. Let cool and then serve. Makes 12 servings.

Bananas Foster
1 cup brown sugar soaked in banana liquor
3 ripe bananas, peeled and sliced
French Vanilla ice cream
E & J Brandy
Banana liquor
Grand Marnier
Directions: Heat 1 shot of each liquor in a skillet. When the liquors are hot, tip the skillet next to a flame to ignite. Add brown sugar and bananas. Cook for 30 - 40 seconds until hot and flame goes out. Serve hot over 1 scoop of ice cream. Yield: 6 servings

Swiss Style Chocolate Fondue
Ingredients
3 (3-ounce) bars Toblerone
½ cup heavy cram
4 tablespoons of Grand Marnier or Triple Sec liqueur
Directions: Break the Toblerone into separate triangular pieces.
Combine all the ingredients in a saucepan or small double broiler. Stir
over low heat until the chocolate is melted and smooth. Serve in your
favorite fondue dish with low heat. Serve with fresh strawberries,
grapes, bananas slices, Angel food cake or ladyfingers

Basic Crepes
Ingredients:
1 cup all-purpose flour
1/2 cup water
1/4 teaspoon salt
2 tablespoons butter, melted
2 eggs
1/2 cup milk
Directions:
In a large mixing bowl, whisk together the flour and the eggs. Gradually
add in the milk and water, stirring to combine. Add the salt and butter;
beat until smooth.
Heat a lightly oiled griddle or frying pan over medium high heat. Pour
or scoop the batter onto the griddle, using approximately 1/4 cup for
each crepe. Tilt the pan with a circular motion so that the batter coats
the surface evenly. Cook the crepe for about 2 minutes, until the
bottom is light brown. Loosen with a spatula, turn and cook the other
side. Serve hot.

Chocolate Cup
Ingredients
Water balloons
Melting chocolate
Directions: Inflate, tie ends and freeze balloons.
Slowly heat chocolate and melt. Slowly dip bottom half of balloons in chocolate to cover surface to make a cup. Cool or freeze. Pop balloons and remove carefully from chocolate coating. Fill with mousse, ice cream or whatever you like.

Chocolate Parfait (Low Fat)
Ingredients
1 (1.4 oz.) package fat-free, sugar-free chocolate instant pudding mix
2 cups 1% low-fat milk
½ cup light sour cream
1 (8 oz) fat-free frozen whipped topping, thawed and divided
¾ cup chocolate graham cracker crumbs (4 cracker sheets)
1 Tbsp. Freshly grated chocolate
Directions: Whisk together first 3 ingredients in a bowl until blended and smooth.
Fold in 1 ½ cups whipped topping. Spoon 1 Tbsp. Crumbs into each of 6 (4 oz.) glasses, and top with 1/3 cup pudding mixture. Repeat layers with remaining crumbs and pudding mixture. Top each parfait evenly with remaining whipped topping and grated chocolate. Cover and chill at least 1 hour. Yield: Make 6 servings

Diabetic Banana Oatmeal Cookies
Ingredients
3 ripe bananas
1/3 cup salad oil
2 cups uncooked quick-cooking oats
1-1/2 cups chopped walnuts
1 teaspoon vanilla
3/4 teaspoon salt

Directions: Preheat oven to 350 F. In a large bowl, mash the bananas and then add all the other ingredients. Drop rounded teaspoons of cookie dough onto an ungreased cookie sheet. Bake for 20-25 minutes. Remove from oven and place on a wire rack to cool. (Note: The cookies are tastier the following day.) Yield: 1 dozen cookies

English Fruit Trifle
1 cup Amaretto liqueur
18 lady finger cookies
5 kiwi fruit, peeled and sliced thin
4 ounces mandarin orange segments, drained
2 cups blueberry filling
1 pint fresh strawberries or seasonal fruit
10 cups chilled pastry cream (recipe follows)

Pastry Cream
Ingredients
4 cups sugar
10 cups milk
1/4 cup corn starch
8 eggs
1/4 cup vanilla flavoring
Directions: Prepare the pastry cream: Combine sugar, milk and corn syrup in sauce pan. Cook over medium heat for 5 minutes. In a bowl beat eggs with a fork and add vanilla flavoring. Mix well. Add a small amount of hot milk mixture to eggs, stirring rapidly to prevent lumping. Add egg mixture to hot milk in sauce pan and continue to cook over medium heat until thickened. Stir continually. When thickened, remove from heat and chill.

Gingered Pumpkin Pie
Ingredients
1 cup cooked, mashed pumpkin
¾ cup evaporated skimmed milk
½ cup unsweetened applesauce
¼ cup sugar
¼ cup reduced-calorie maple syrup
2 egg whites
1 egg
2 teaspoons cornstarch
1 ½ teaspoons pumpkin pie spice
Vegetable cooking spray
8 (2 inch-diameter) gingersnaps
2 tablespoons gingersnap crumbs
Directions: Combine first 9 ingredients in a large bowl; beat at medium speed of an electric mixer until well blended. Coat a 9-inch pie plate with cooking spray. Cut gingersnaps in half, using a bread knife. Line side of pie plate with cookie halves, cut side down. Spoon pumpkin mixture into prepared pie plate. Sprinkle with gingersnap crumbs. Bake at 400 degrees for 15 minutes. Reduce heat to 350 degrees; bake an additional 20 minutes or until knife inserted in center comes out clean. Yield: 8

Elvis's Peach Cobbler
January 8th is Elvis Presley's Birthday and if you know me you know I am a big Elvis fan. Elvis loved to eat as we could tell in his later years. Southern cooking was his favorite, most when they think Elvis they think Grilled Peanut Butter and Banana sandwich. This may be true but he also loves his Memphis BBQ and Peach Cobbler. So here is an easy recipe that you can make to celebrate the "Kings" birthday
Ingredients
1 large can (29 ounces) sliced peaches in syrup
1 medium can (15 ounces) sliced peaches in syrup

1/2 to 1 teaspoon ground cinnamon
1/4 teaspoon nutmeg
1 tablespoon cornstarch
1 cup sugar
1 cup flour
1 1/2 teaspoons baking powder
1/2 teaspoon salt
1 egg, beaten
6 tablespoons melted butter, divided
2 tablespoons milk
2 teaspoons sugar mixed with 1/4 teaspoon ground cinnamon
Directions: Drain peaches, reserving syrup in a measuring cup. If you don't have 1 cup of syrup, add water to make 1 cup; set aside. Toss peaches with spices. Combine 3/4 cup of the syrup with the cornstarch; stir into peaches. Arrange peaches in an 11x7-inch baking dish. Into a bowl, sift the sugar, flour, baking powder, and salt. Stir in the beaten egg, 1/4 cup of the reserved syrup, 1/4 of milk, and 4 tablespoons of the melted butter. Spoon the batter evenly over the peaches. Drizzle with remaining butter then sprinkle with the cinnamon sugar.
Bake in a preheated 350° oven for about 35 to 45 minutes, until top is nicely browned. Of course to really top this off right serve the hot cobbler with a scoop of Vanilla Ice Cream.

Fresh Apple Cake
Ingredients
4 cups diced fresh apples
2 cups sugar
1/2 cup Wesson oil
1 cup nuts
2 eggs, well beaten
2 teaspoons vanilla
2 cups flour

2 teaspoons baking soda
2 teaspoons cinnamon
1 teaspoon salt
Directions: Preheat oven to 350 degrees. In a large bowl, add apples and sugar and mix to coat apples well. Add oil, nuts, eggs and vanilla. Mix well. In a separate bowl mix flour, baking soda, cinnamon and salt. Add to apple mixture and mix well. Pour into a greased 9" x 13" x 2" pan and bake f or one hour. Remove and cool on wire rack.

Peach Crisp
This old fashioned dessert is good served warm or cold.
Ingredients
4 cups peeled, sliced peaches or
canned sliced peaches, drained
1/4 cup orange juice
4 teaspoons firmly packed brown sugar
2 teaspoons lemon juice
1 teaspoon cinnamon
Non stick spray or coating
1/2 cup oats (quick or old fashioned)
1 tablespoon firmly packed brown sugar

Directions: Preheat oven to 375 degrees.
Spray 8-inch by 8-inch baking dish with non-stick coating. Combine first 5 ingredients and mix well.
Arrange peach mixture in baking dish. Combine remaining ingredients and sprinkle over peach mixture. Bake for 30 minutes, or until peaches are tender if using fresh, and topping is lightly browned. Yield:8 servings

Pineapple & Fresh Fruit with Strawberry Yogurt Dressing
Ingredients
1 whole pineapple, cut into quarters
1/2 cup fresh strawberries, cleaned
2 cups fat free plain yogurt
1/2 cup grapes, cleaned
1/2 cup cantaloupe, cleaned, peeled and cubed
4 tablespoons strawberry gelatin
Directions: Place pineapple on plate with stem up. In a medium size mixing bowl, add fresh cut fruit. In a small mixing bowl add yogurt and gelatin; mix well until yogurt turns full red color. Add yogurt mixture to fresh fruit and mix well. Gently fold in dressing so as not to bruise fruit. Place fresh fruit on plate next to pineapple and garnish with a mint leaf. Yield: 4 servings

Rum Balls
Valery's favorite dessert
Ingredients
2 cups vanilla wafer crumbs
1 cup sweetened, shredded coconut
1 to 2-1/2 cups confectioner's sugar
2 tablespoons light corn syrup
1/3 cup rum
Directions: Prepare wafers in food processor. Combine crumbs, coconut, 1 cup sugar, corn syrup and rum in a bowl. Mix well. Shape into firm balls 3/4 inch in diameter. Sift remaining sugar onto waxed paper. Roll the rum balls in the sugar. Store until needed. Yield: 50 rum balls

Macadamia Nut Tuiles
Ingredients
1/4 cup (1/2 stick) unsalted butter
1/2 cup brown sugar, packed
1/4 cup light corn syrup
1/2 cup all-purpose flour
pinch of salt
1/2 cup toasted macadamia nuts, finely ground
Direction: To make the tuiles: In the bowl of an electric mixer, cream the butter with the sugar. Add corn syrup and mix well. Combine the flour and salt and beat into the butter mixture. Stir in the nuts with a wooden spoon. Preheat the oven to 350 F. Line cookie sheets with parchment paper. Lightly draw 3-inch circles on the paper and spread the batter as thinly as possible within the area of each circle, smoothing with the back of a spoon. Bake for 3 to 5 minutes or until golden. Remove from oven and remove a tuile cookie with a spatula, pressing the cookie over the bottom of an inverted small bowl or custard cup. Repeat with remaining tuiles; if they become brittle, place them back in the oven for a moment to re-warm them. Let cool. Set aside.

Sicilian Cannoli
The true Sicilian dessert for all special occasions
Filling Shells
Ingredients
3 cups ricotta cheese
3 cups all-purpose flour
1-1/4 cups sugar
1/4 cup sugar
2 teaspoons vanillas extract
1/4 teaspoon salt
1 tablespoon Marsala wine or sherry
1/2 cup dried fruit, finely chopped

1/4 cup semi-sweet chocolate pieces
Directions: Combine first 4 filling ingredients and beat until smooth. Add the dried fruit and chocolate pieces. Mix together well and chill. Cut into pastry blender until pieces are size of peas. Add 3 tablespoons of shortening. Stir in 2 eggs, well beaten. Blend in 2 tablespoons of white vinegar, 2 tablespoons of cold water and turn dough onto lightly floured surface and knead. Wrap in waxed paper and chill for 30 minutes. Add 3 cups of oil to deep sauce pan and heat to 360 degrees. Cut cardboard into oval pattern 6 x 4-1/2 inches. Roll chilled dough 1/8 inch thick on floured surface. Cut dough into oval patterns using cardboard. Wrap dough loosely around cannoli tubes, lapping over opposite edges. Seal edges by brushing with slightly beaten egg whites. Press edges together to seal. Fry about 8 minutes or until golden brown. Drain on paper towels. Cool slightly and remove tubes. When ready to serve, fill with ricotta filling. Sprinkle ends of cannoli with chocolate chips. Sprinkle cannoli with powdered sugar. Yield: 10 servings

Strawberries Romanoff
Ingredients
 2 pints Strawberries
1/2 cup Sugar (or 1/4 cup sugar + 3 packets Sweet 'N Low)
1/3 cup Grand Marnier
1 pint Vanilla non-fat frozen yogurt
1 (1.3 oz package) Dream Whip (prepared -- 2 cups)
1/4 teaspoon Almond extract
Directions: Gently wash berries in cold water. Drain on paper towels; hull. Turn into serving bowl. Sprinkle with sugar and Grand Marnier; toss. Chill 1 hour, stirring occasionally. Let frozen yogurt soften in refrigerator about 1 hour. Make Dream Whip with skim milk and vanilla as package directs. Fold in almond extract. Gently fold in Dream Whip, softened yogurt, and strawberries together. Serve at once in stemmed dessert goblets. Yield: Serves 8

Tiramisu Parfait

Ingredients

4 ounces of Strong Espresso (or substitute 2 teaspoons of instant coffee in ½ cup of water.)

2 ounces of Italian Brandy

4 Egg Yolks

2 tablespoons of Sugar

2 Egg whites

2 cups of Macscarpone Cheese (may substitute ricotta or cream cheese)

30 small Savioardi, or 15 broken in half (Italian Lady Fingers)

3 ounces of bittersweet chocolate broken into 1/4-inch pieces

3 ounces of milk chocolate, shaved or grated

6 large wine goblets

Directions: Mix coffee and brandy together and set aside. Over a double boiler, beat egg yolks and sugar until mixture lightens in color and forms ribbons (i.e. halfway to zabaglione). Allow to cool 5 minutes. Meanwhile, beat egg whites to stiff peaks. Fold mascarpone into egg yolk mixture one quarter at a time. Fold mascarpone mixture into egg whites and set aside. Lay savoiardi along edges of wine goblets all the way to the bottom, lining the entire glass (while keeping 6 savoiardi for later use). Using a pastry brush, and paint the cookies with the espresso/brandy mixture. Fill each goblet one-third full with mascarpone mixture and sprinkle with broken chocolate. Lay one savoiardi across center and paint with coffee mixture. Fill each goblet with remaining mascarpone mixture, topping each with shaved chocolate.

Lay one savoiardi in each goblet and paint with espresso mixture.

Zeppole
Fritters for Saint Joseph's Day
Ingredients
For the dough:
2 1/2 cups (250 g) flour, sifted
An equal volume of water
A pinch of salt
A pot of olive oil for frying (you can use other oils if need be)
1/2 cup (about 125 ml) white wine
Directions: For the dredging: 3 teaspoons powdered cinnamon mixed with 1 cup (200 g) sugar Set the water and wine to heat, and when bubbles form on the bottom of the pot (it's shouldn't come to a full boil) add the flour in one fell swoop and stir constantly with a wooden spoon. When the dough comes out of the pot in a single piece remove it from the fire to a lightly oiled marble work surface and work it, pounding it with a rolling pin, for about 10 minutes so as to make it smooth and homogeneous. Roll the dough into snakes about as thick as your little finger, cut them into 8-inch (20 cm) lengths, and pinch the ends together to make rings. Heat the oil and fry the zeppole a few at a time, pricking them with a skewer as they fry, so the dough will bubble out and they'll become crunchier and more golden. Drain them on an absorbent paper and dredge them in the cinnamon-and-sugar mixture. They're good hot or cold. If you choose to dip them in a honey mixture, forgo the sugar and cinnamon mentioned above.Prepare instead:
3/4 cup (250 g) honey
2/3 cup (125 g) sugar
1 pinch powdered cinnamon
1/2 teaspoon vanilla extract
3 tablespoons water
Diavolilli (colored candy bits; she calls for 50 g, or 2 ounces by weight)
Make the zeppole and keep them warm

Mix the honey, water and sugar, and cook the syrup until the fine thread stage (squeeze a drop between thumb and forefinger, then separate them; fine threads that break easily should form).
Lower the flame to an absolute minimum, stir in the cinnamon and the vanilla, and dip the zeppole 2 or 3 at a time, removing them with a fork and laying them on the serving dish. When you have finished dipping, sprinkle the zeppole with diavolilli, pour the remaining syrup over them, and serve hot.

Punch
Ingredients
1 large block of ice
8 ounces orange juice
8 ounces lemonade
8 ounces limeade
8 ounces pineapple juice
8 ounce can crushed pineapple
1 quart line sherbet
16 ounces water
2 large bottles ginger ale
Directions: In a large punch bowl or serving bowl, place block of ice. Add all ingredients to the bowl, except for the ginger ale, and mix together well. Add ginger ale just before serving. Yield: 10 servings

Chilly Orange Drink
Ingredients
1/2 cup chilled orange drink
1/2 cup orange sherbet
3/4 cup chilled ginger ale
Directions: Pour 1/4 cup of orange drink into each glass. Next put half of the sherbet into each glass. Finally, add half of the ginger ale to each glass. Drink up!

Always remember we should learn our heritage but also learn and respect those of other heritages.

Life is short!
Break the rules!
Forgive quickly!
Kiss slowly!
Love truly!
Laugh uncontrollably!
Never regret anything
that made you smile!

"Life's journey is not to arrive at the grave safely in a well-preserved body, but rather to skid in sideways, totally worn out, shouting, 'Holy shit......What a ride!'"

Cajun Eggs
Chicken and Sausage Jambalaya
Chuck Wagon Chili
Grilled Fillet Mignon
Steak Maitre'D
Shrimp Diane
Grilled Shrimp w/ Mango Sauce
Mango Salsa
Shrimp Galveston
Shrimp Scampi
Shrimp Etoufee
Scallops in Wine Sauce
Halibut Steak
Roast Turkey
Steak Luzon
Roasted Quail
Yankee Pot Roast
Spambalaya
Spam Wellington
Meatless Jambalaya
Smokin' Barbeque Pork Chili
Rub

Italian……87
Aunt Babe's Spinach Pizza
Bagna Calda
Braised Short Ribs
Black Pepper Fettuccini
Chicken Cacciatore
Chicken Marsala
Chicken Parmesan
Sicilian Chicken Pasta
Papa Joe's Spaghetti Sauce
Nana's Eggplant

Roasted Chicken w/Prosciutto
Popeyed Pesto Chicken
Ciabatta Deli Sandwiches
Eggplant Bayou
Fettuccini Alfredo
Fettuccini Jambalaya
Italian Style Meatballs
Pasta Primavera
Linguine of the Sea
Poached Salmon over Pesto
Pasta
Veal Picatta
New Years Day Italian Style
Pancakes

Mexican……114
Chili Relleno Casserole
Enchilada Pie
The History of Fajita's
Fajitas
Lime Marinade
Mexican Salad Roll-up
Thanksgiving Turkey Taco's

Asian….123
Chicken Lettuce Wraps
Chicken Lettuce Wraps for
Kids Thai Chicken Wraps
Kalua Pork
Pork Pot Stickers
Thai Chicken Wraps
Honey Chicken Wrap Marinade
Pad Thai
Pho Bo Soup
Honey-Soy Broiled Salmon

Tangelo Pork Stir-Fry

Apple Stuffing
Baked Artichoke
Barbeque Beans
Black-Eyed Peas
Broccoli Cooked in Wine
Chanukah Latkes
Creamed Onions with Lima Beans
Golden Hominy
Giblet Gravy
Herbed Potato Pie
Lemon Sauce
Pizza Sauce
Potato Kugel
Potato Pancakes
Potato, Turnip and Chard Sauté
Risotto
Spanish Corn
Special Rice
Sweet Potato Bake

Aunt Mary's Poppy Seed Cake
Aunt Jean's Chocolate Chip Cookies
Easy Baklava
Banana Foster
Swiss Style Chocolate Fondue
Chocolate Cup
Chocolate Parfait (Low Fat)
Diabetic Banana Oatmeal Cookies

English Fruit Trifle
Pastry Cream
Gingered Pumpkin Pie
Elvis's Peach Cobbler
Fresh Apple Cake
Peach Crisp
Pineapple & Fresh Fruit with Strawberry Yogurt Dressing
Rum Balls
Macadamia Nut Tuiles
Sicilian Cannolli
Strawberry Romanoff
Tiramisu Parfait
Zeppole
Punch
Chilly Orange Drink